TETO

AND OTHER PETZOLDT ANECDOTES

BY
PAUL PETZOLDT

Papa, Happy 57th, I think you
will be able to relate to this
old timer, he's both a great
climber and writer. Tara,
Nikki

ICS BOOKS, INC.
MERRILLVILLE, INDIANA

TETON TALES   And Other Petzoldt Anecdotes
Copyright © 1995 By Paul Petzoldt
Cover Photo: (From left to right) Geraldine Lucas, Paul Petzoldt, Ike Powell, Alan Budge, and Jack Crawford at the summit of the Grand Teton. in 1924. This was sixteen-year-old Paul Petzoldt's second ascent of the "peerless peak." (The Alan Budge Collection)
Grand Teton Photo by K.C. Muscolino
Back Cover Photo by K.C. Muscolino
10 9 8 7 6 5 4 3 2 1

All rights reserved, including the right to reproduce this book or portions thereof in any form or by any means, electronic or mechanical, including photocopying, recording, unless authorization is obtained, in writing, from the publisher. All inquiries should be addressed to ICS Books, Inc., 1370 East 86th Place, Merrillville, Indiana 46410.

Published by:
ICS BOOKS, Inc.
1370 E. 86th Place
Merrillville, IN 46410
800-541-7323

All ICS titles are printed on 50% recycled paper from pre-consumer waste. All sheets are processed without using acid.

LIBRARY OF CONGRESS CATALOGING-IN-PUBLICATION DATA
Petzoldt, Paul.
    Teton tales / Paul Petzoldt.
        p.   cm.
    ISBN 1-57034-015-3
    I. Title.
PS3566.E898T48   1995
818' .5403--dc20
    [B]   95-24428
                                                  CIP

DEDICATION

*I would like to dedicate this book to my wife
Ginnie, who encouraged me to record my stories.*

IN APPRECIATION

*Special thanks to Kevin "Butch" Cassidy, who was as
successful and relentless in helping me produce this book
as the original Butch Cassidy was at robbing trains.*

CONTENTS

ACKNOWLEDGMENTS   VI

INTRODUCTION   VII

CHAPTER 1: I AIN'T LOST NOTHIN' UP THERE   1

CHAPTER 2: THE KID GROWS UP   35

CHAPTER 3: HOW TEPEE'S GLACIER GOT ITS NAME   57

CHAPTER 4: THE LAST OF THE OLD WEST   69

CHAPTER 5: LIFE IN THE HOLE   85

CHAPTER 6: BARON EXUM   93

CHAPTER 7: OF FISH AND BEARS   100

CHAPTER 8: DUDES   114

CHAPTER 9: DEMON RUM   122

CHAPTER 10: BRING 'EM BACK ALIVE   127

CHAPTER 11: DON'T BUCK THE ODDS   143

CHAPTER 12: THE LEGEND OF JOHN EMERY   153

CHAPTER 13: FROM WYOMING TO WINDSOR CASTLE   159

CHAPTER 14: THE FIRST WINTER ASCENT OF THE GRAND   169

CHAPTER 15: THE NORTH FACE   179

CHAPTER 16: PLANE WRECK ON MOUNT MORAN   187

CHAPTER 17: TALON FINGERS AND WILD EYES   199

EPILOGUE   212

ACKNOWLEDGMENTS

There are many people and institutions whose hard work and patience have helped make this book possible. I would like to thank them here.

I would like to thank Mike Demmings and Malinda Fishman for spending time with me in Maine collecting some of the original research that went into the book.

Thanks go out to two friends who helped with memories and sound advice: Raye Ringholz, whose efforts were responsible for the success of NOLS and for establishing women as leaders in the outdoors; and Caine Alder, confidant and Petzoldt historian.

Grand Teton National Park was very cooperative, and I would like to thank Superintendent Jack Neckels and his staff, especially Linda Olson, Reny Jackson, and Mary McKinney. Thanks also to all the previous Grand Teton National Park superintendents, especially Superintendents Whitcraft and Smith, the first in their position to view mountaineers as sane people. Superintendent Charles Smith was the first to climb the Grand Teton, personally guided by me, and accompanied by a reluctant park assistant.

The University of Wyoming's American Heritage Center deserves thanks for providing photos and Billy Owen's records and diaries, and thanks to Marla Peterson for collecting research out West. Thanks to the Teton County Historical Society in Jackson for photos and old newspaper articles.

Two sources we called upon again and again were Orin and Lorraine Bonney's *The Grand Controversy*, and *Mountaineering in the Tetons, The Pioneer Period 1898-1940*, written by Fritiof Fryxell, an authority on the Tetons from whom I learned a tremendous amount, and by Phil Smith, my first guide, who managed my park concession while I was off climbing in Switzerland and the Himalayas.

Thanks go out to Glenn Exum for his remembrances and his photos. Glenn, a close friend and fellow Idahoan, helped to develop the Teton Guiding Service through the Petzoldt-Exum School of American Mountaineering.

Lisa Wogan deserves special thanks for her efforts at organizing and editing throughout the course of the project, especially during the crucial final stages. Her good judgment prevented my tendency to self-destruct.

INTRODUCTION

"This book is not an historical monument. This is what I heard. This is what I saw. This is what people said."
— Paul Petzoldt

At some point during the one and a half years I have known Paul and helped him with this book, the thought came to me that perhaps Paul had crossed paths with Ernest Hemingway. The more I thought about it, the more I pictured the scene: in a bar, fighting over a beautiful woman, then forgetting about the woman as they shared a few drinks, slapped each other on the back, and traded war stories.

One day, Hemingway came up in our conversation. I was probably telling Paul how much I admired Hemingway's lean style of writing and precise word choice when Paul casually said, "I met him once."

"Where?" I asked.

"In a bar," he said. "He invited me up to go fishing at his ranch in Sun Valley." Now this was my favorite author he was talking about, the man who had inspired me to run down a narrow street with angry bulls. I was ready for a story.

"What happened?" I asked. "What did you talk about?"

"Not much," Paul said. "We didn't talk about politics or anything. We just fished." And I figured that was just what they should have done.

Few Americans have spanned this century with as much flair as Paul Petzoldt. He has embraced life in an open, no-regrets, passionate way that is the soil from which memorable stories spring.

When Horace Greeley said, "Go West, young man, and grow up with the country," Paul took him seriously. Hell, Greeley might as well have been talking directly to Paul. Regardless, it was still a young country in many ways when Paul and his family packed up and left their corn farm in Iowa for the promise of potato-raising west of the Rockies in Idaho. World War I had just ended, and the United States had lost some of her innocence, but not all of it.

Since then, Paul has indeed grown up with the country.

The stories in this book trace his trail full of switchbacks from the Tetons to Toledo, where he worked as a waiter in a city he describes as a "gangster's paradise"; from Wyoming to Windsor Castle; from Mount Moran to the Matterhorn; and everywhere in between.

Traveling was his hobby, but the Tetons and Jackson's Hole were his home. As far as he roamed, he always returned to the mountains where he made his name as a bold teenage guide. It is in those mountains, and in the valley below them, and in the lives of the people who lived there when it was still "the last of the Old West" that most of this book is set.

Through all his wilderness adventures, Paul has remained a step ahead of the conservation movement, setting the example for others. While operating a hunting camp in Jackson's Hole in the thirties, he suggested at an annual Wyoming Outfitter's Association meeting that if hunters were going to leave their trash in the woods, they should at least hide it in the willows so others didn't have to look at it. He was almost laughed out of the room.

Undaunted, Paul set his own standards of behavior in the outdoors, standards that form the basis of what people today call expedition behavior and minimum-impact camping.

In the sixties, while serving as chief instructor for the first American Outward Bound school, Paul was called before Congress to testify about the Wilderness Bill. The bill was going to set aside millions of acres to be preserved, with provisions that much of it remain accessible to the American public. Paul called for an educational component to the bill, recognizing that the bill would quickly become meaningless if the very people the land was being preserved for were unknowingly destroying it.

When he saw that no educational measures were added by Congress, Paul took matters into his own hands. He formed the National Outdoor Leadership School (NOLS) in 1965 to teach others, mostly young people, the outdoor ethic he had been refining for thirty years. NOLS was a huge success, but Paul still felt his message wasn't reaching a wide enough audience. In the mid-seventies, he was the driving force behind the establishment of the Wilderness Education Association (WEA), an organization dedicated to bringing outdoor education to colleges and universities across the country.

The expanse of Paul's influence is hard to determine because of the grassroots nature of his approach. He brought people out into the field, explained to them his philosophy, and taught them the techniques needed to implement it. Then he taught them how to teach others. His lessons have been simple: Know where you are going, watch your step, look around the bend, and pay attention to what you have left behind.

It has been both an honor and a lot of fun working with Paul on this book. In a time when stories and their tellers are disappearing as fast as television and video can blot them out, this collection provides an often humorous and clearly invaluable look at a piece of this country's history. These stories are a celebration of Paul's unique life. He is truly one of a kind. Many people call him a visionary, and he certainly lives up to that. But I like to refer to him as an actionary. There are those who see what is ahead and those who shape it. Paul is one of the few who does both.

— *Kevin "Butch" Cassidy*

All my life, people have asked the question, directly or indirectly, "Why in the hell do you climb mountains?"

I can't explain this to other people. I love the physical exertion. I love the wind. I love the storms. I love the fresh air. I love the companionship in the outdoors. I love the reality. I love the change. I love the rejuvenating spirit. I love to feel oneness with nature. I'm hungry; I enjoy eating. I get thirsty; I enjoy the clear water. I enjoy being warm at night when it's cold outside. All those simple things are extremely enjoyable because, gosh, you're feeling them, you're living them, your senses are really feeling. I can't explain it.

— Paul Petzoldt, 1976

CHAPTER ONE

I AIN'T LOST
NOTHIN' UP THERE

"No previous attempt on the Teton has been attended by such physical hardship and suffering as these young men endured, and had they not possessed the courage, fortitude and determination that mark the true mountaineer, they never would have reached the summit of Wyoming's peerless peak."
— Jackson Hole Courier, *July 31, 1924*

I

The Snake River ran through the center of the valley with cottonwoods hugging its banks, pressed there by the outlines of hayfields and ranches. Amid the wildflowers covering the hillside stood a sign that read HOWDY PARTNER, YONDER LIES JACKSON'S HOLE, THE LAST OF THE OLD WEST.

It was the summer of 1924, and I was at the top of Teton Pass in Wyoming. "The old tin lizzy ain't got no brakes," Nephi said. This snapped me back to reality. Nephi was the kind person who picked up Ralph Herron and me as we were leaving Victor, Idaho, hoping to get a ride over Teton Pass into Jackson. Ralph, my friend and traveling companion, was seventeen, a year older than I. We had started from Twin Falls with the idea of going to visit his relatives, George Kelly and Dick Winger, who were living in Jackson. Our plans did not go far beyond that.

But our lives changed when we rounded a bend near Rexburg and saw the Tetons. Suddenly we had another goal. We were going to climb the Grand Teton.

1

In that instant, it became our ambition. Now we were on an expedition, a real expedition, the kind that we had read about and dreamed about. We were going into Jackson's Hole and we were going to climb the Grand Teton.

Nephi, with his Model T Ford, had plucked us from the dusty road leaving Victor and had brought us to the top of the pass, but not without some problems. The Ford heated up periodically, and each little stream that crossed the road was a source of new water to pour in the radiator that gushed like a miniature Old Faithful. Nephi and his car were a determined pair, but before we reached the top of the pass the car stopped moving forward.

I knew Model T Fords so I understood what was happening when Nephi turned the car around and backed up the rest of the way to the top. The gas tanks in Model Ts were located under the windshield, above the carburetor, which was further forward in the engine. On a steep upward grade, the carburetor leveled out with the gas tank, so there wasn't enough gravity to feed the gas into the carburetor. When the car was turned around it worked fine. This was, of course, before the days of fuel pumps.

On the way up we told Nephi we were going to climb the Grand Teton, and he looked at us as if we were crazy.

"Climb the Grand Teton!" he said. "You'll be killed. I've been up there hunting bighorn sheep and I don't believe any human being can get to the top of the Grand Teton."

Ralph was an extremely intelligent and well-read young man. "Well," Ralph said, "I have read that Billy Owen climbed to the top of the Grand Teton in 1898."

"That's what some people say, but most people don't believe it," Nephi said. "I guess he probably did, because I know Frank Peterson, who has a ranch over there in Jackson's Hole, and he said he went up there to the top with Billy Owen in 1898. I guess if Frank Peterson said they got up there, they got up there. But, by God, I ain't lost nothin' up there and it's no place for you kids. You'll never come back alive."

For the moment we let the subject drop. We had more pressing matters to attend to, like the prospect of getting down the steep mountain road with its many hairpin turns.

Paul (left), nineteen , with Ralph Herron, his partner for Paul's first ascent of the Grand Teton in 1924. The photo was taken April 1927. (Violet Herrick Collection)

"This sonofabitch don't have any brakes," Nephi reminded us. He got out of the car, took out an ax and a log chain, and proceeded to cut down a fairly good-sized pine tree next to the road. He was a good axman, and chips spun around and covered the ground until the tree fell. Then he backed his Ford up near the tree, fastened the log chain around the axle and around the tree, and said, "Jump in." Down we went, down Teton Pass, dragging the tree with all its limbs smoothing the road behind us in a cloud of dust and holding us back from speeding over the cliffs to eternity.

Finally, near the bottom, the car stopped and Nephi had us look back up the hill. Near the top of a mountain high above Teton Pass we saw a big open slope about half a mile wide. It wasn't a real mountain like the Tetons, but it was bigger than the ones we had back in Idaho. Only young saplings grew in the open slope, which narrowed down into a funnel, and I wondered why there was no timber. Nephi answered my unspoken question.

"That's the biggest damned avalanche in the country," Nephi said. "Those trees you see growing on the slope are too young to be knocked over by the snow. They're just bent down. In a few years the avalanche will tear out their roots and carry 'em down to some of these big piles you see at the bottom of the hill."

"What starts the avalanche?" Ralph asked.

"It could be a lot of things," Nephi said. "The wind blows from the west and forms a big cornice of snow up on top of that ridge. Sometimes a piece of that cornice builds up so much it breaks off, and that would start it. They say when you're in avalanche country you shouldn't shout, because maybe your voice will start it. I'm not so sure about that, but I am sure that you have to be damned careful when you come past this place in the winter with your mail sled or your sled bringing supplies over from the railroad in Victor. If you're in front of its path when the snow slides, there ain't no hope for you."

"How often does it run?" Ralph asked.

"You never can tell, but it runs two or three times almost every year," Nephi said.

A short time later we stopped again near a ledge. We unchained the tree and helped Nephi roll it over the cliff into a little canyon. As I looked down, I saw that our tree was not the first to be used to hold back vehicles with poor brakes coming down Teton Pass.

As we reached the bottom of the pass, we sped through the little town of Wilson and crossed the Snake River bridge. "This is the Snake River," Nephi said, and we got out to take a look. The river was smooth going under the bridge, but the current was quick. We could see riffles and rapids above and below where we stood. So this was the river of the big trout that people around Twin Falls talked about catching. It looked like it was in flood.

"Now up there, if you look way up the valley, you can see that ridge of mountains," Nephi said. "Right there in the middle, the highest one, is the Grand Teton. You see how steep it is and how steep those snowfields and glaciers are. I think you kids would be well advised to stick to the lower slopes if you go up there. I want you to come back alive," Nephi said.

We got back in the car and after rounding a couple buttes, found ourselves in the little town of Jackson. It was even smaller than we had imagined. We stopped on the east side of the town square near Mercill's, a general merchandise store and grocery. Down the street a ways was the Jackson State Bank, a hardware store, a drugstore, and the Crabtree Hotel. Nestled in the corner of the square was the local saloon and pool hall where a person could usually find a poker game, Nephi told us. Across the street from the saloon was an old hotel. Around the corner to the west was a livery stable where people kept their horses when they rode into town. A couple of cars were parked on the dusty street, and a handful of people were browsing amid the storefronts. It was quiet.

Nephi pointed to a nearby valley. "That's Cash Creek coming down there," he said. "George Kelly lives up there by the graveyard in a log house. If you just go thataway and then along the hill, you'll come to his place." We thanked Nephi profusely for his help, and said if we climbed the Grand Teton we'd be very careful and we expected to come back alive.

"Well, I think you should give it up," he said. "I think you should give up that idea." With that we parted company.

Soon we were out to the Kellys'. They greeted us cordially and asked about their friends and relatives back in Newton, Iowa, Ralph's hometown. Ralph filled them in on family matters. Afterwards, they showed us where we could sleep out in their barn using some hay for padding. We stored our meager belongings, which included two patchwork quilts I had taken from my home in Twin Falls. Most of the time we slept under the stars, and the quilts were our sleeping bags. We did not have money for hotels. As a matter of fact, we didn't have money for much else either.

As the sun was starting to sink in the west, a vehicle pulled up to the entrance to the Kelly home. An impressive figure got out and walked toward the house. He was dressed like a real cowboy, wearing a Stetson hat, Pendleton pants, with well-shined boots. He also had a holstered pistol hanging low from a wide leather belt around his waist. Little leather loops on the outer surface of the belt were filled with cartridges, probably .44 caliber, ammunition heavy enough to knock down a moose. Because of their shape, we sometimes called holstered pistols hoglegs.

We marveled at seeing a real westerner, not a make-believe cowboy, but one of the real ones. "I wonder what the sheriff wants up here?" George asked his wife just before the stranger reached the door.

The cowboy smiled and spoke directly to us. "Young men, it's all over town that you two are going to try and climb the Grand Teton. Is that right?"

"We're going to try and climb it and we think we'll get to the top," we said.

"Well, that's a very serious undertaking. I think that you boys should reconsider. And how about your parents, do they know about this?" he asked.

Ralph didn't say anything, but I told him my mother wouldn't mind. The sheriff took George aside, and they spoke for several minutes out of earshot. Before turning to leave, the sheriff came back over to us and said, "Have a good visit, young fellas, and welcome to Jackson's Hole."

"We'll take care of these young men and we'll keep you informed as to what they're going to do," George told the sheriff.

It wasn't long before another gentleman came down the road. He was rather small and had a gait that was half a run. He introduced himself to George. "I'm Billy Owen," he said. "I'm visiting here for the first time in many years and heard a rumor around town that these two young men are going to climb the Grand Teton."

"Are you the Billy Owen who climbed the Grand Teton in 1898?" Ralph asked.

"I sure am," Mr. Owen said. "And I think if you boys are going up there we should have a talk. As a matter of fact, I'm very interested in your adventure. How about coming down to the Crabtree Hotel and being my guests for breakfast at eight o'clock tomorrow morning. Would you do that?"

We said sure, we'd be there. And so ended our first day in Jackson's Hole.

That night, as we stretched out on our hay mattresses between our patchwork quilts, we were too excited to sleep. Not only were we on a real expedition, but we had met Billy Owen, the first man to climb the Grand Teton. He was interested in our expedition, and we hoped he would give us pointers on how to reach the top. We had no doubt that we would reach the summit in spite of the skepticism of Nephi and the sheriff.

The next morning George woke us. "It's time to get up, boys, if you're going to make that breakfast at eight o'clock. I wish I was going with you. Even the dudes say Mrs. Crabtree is one real good cook. I've heard the expression 'best cook west of the Missouri' and I imagine you'll have a sumptuous breakfast. You don't get an opportunity like that very often, do you?"

Grabbing a pail of water, we filled a basin that sat on top of a stump and washed as quickly as we could. We put on our bib overalls and blue denim shirts, combed our hair, and took off down a hill toward the streets that led to the town square and the Crabtree Hotel. Mr. Owen met us there, sat us down at a table, and introduced us to Mrs. Crabtree by saying, "These two young men are thinking of climbing the Grand Teton."

"Oh, aren't they a little too young for that?" she asked.

We were a little taken aback by that remark, but she smiled at us in goodwill. "Well, what would you boys like for breakfast? How about some bacon and eggs and hotcakes?"

That would be fine with us, we said, and soon she appeared with our steaming breakfast. With our voracious appetites the plates were quickly emptied. But each time, Mrs. Crabtree returned with more pancakes, more eggs, more bacon, and more coffee. Although we were a little embarrassed by our never-ending hunger, Mrs. Crabtree seemed to take it as a compliment.

"Well, it's a nice sunny day," Mr. Owen said after we had gulped our eighth or ninth pancake and had sat back, relaxed, with full stomachs. "Let's go over and sit in front of my cabin in the sun and talk about the climb you want to make."

Mr. Owen's cabin was part of the hotel but one of several one–room cabins set out in back, facing the Tetons. Stretching out in the warm sun with full bellies, talking to Mr. Owen, it was easy to feel like explorers about to embark on a real expedition.

"Have either one of you young men had any mountaineering experience?" he asked.

"I've done some scrambling with Paul near his home on the Snake River Canyon, but I don't have the experience that he has," Ralph said. "He's climbed a lot."

"Well, I have climbed quite a bit," I said. "We lived right on the banks of the Snake River Canyon near Blue Lakes just north of Twin Falls. I have four older brothers who are hunters, fishermen, trappers, and campers and I've learned from them. I've run my own traplines since I was nine, and I spend a lot of time in the canyon trapping and fishing.

"I've climbed all over that canyon. We didn't stick to the steep trails all the time. Sometimes we climbed up and down the steeper parts and one time we even lowered our dogs down over the cliffs with ropes."

"It sounds like you know how to climb," Mr. Owen said.

"Well, I haven't climbed anything like the Grand Teton," I said. "I don't know how to climb on snow, but I've had a lot of practice climbing rocks."

The more Ralph and I talked about climbing the Grand Teton, the more we wanted to do it. "Now if you tell us how you got up there maybe we can make it too," I said to Mr. Owen.

Mr. Owen was impressed by our enthusiasm. "Well, your trip here and your feelings of excitement about climbing the Grand Teton, and going on what you call your own expedition, reminds me of my coming here in 1898 determined to get to the top of the Grand Teton," he said. "One of the reasons I was so intent on it was due to my experience climbing in the Wind River Range. I was bitten by the climbing bug while surveying there. In order to set up our drawing boards to map the terrain, we had to climb to the top of the peaks. That's when I first felt the exhilaration of reaching the summit of a mountain."

Mr. Owen went on to tell us a little bit about the history of Jackson's Hole and the country, and about the circumstances and rumors surrounding a group of government people who came out here in 1872 as part of the Hayden Surveys, claiming to have climbed to the top of the Grand Teton. He told us about an article Nathaniel Langford wrote in *Scribner's Magazine* in 1873 describing Langford's successful climb with James Stevenson. Mr. Owen said the publicity surrounding their climb was very important in securing the appropriations they needed to explore the West.

"The article I read in *Scribner's* raised some serious questions about whether they actually reached the summit," Mr. Owen said. "After I had tried to climb the Grand Teton on several occasions and wasn't able to get to the top from the south side and other sides, I finally went up their route and made it to the Upper Saddle. That's a saddle about five or six hundred feet below the top of the Grand Teton." There he and his companions reached a point where they couldn't go any higher because they were blocked by a great cliff that they didn't have the ability to climb.

He told us how, on his first trip up there, he had gone off to the side to find what's called the Enclosure, where someone had placed some rocks in a circle several feet across. This pinnacle was accurately described in the 1873 article, so Mr. Owen knew that Langford and Stevenson had made it at least that high.

"A rumor got out all over the region, however, that when the climbers from the Langford and Stevenson party came back to camp they said they had gotten to the top of the highest pinnacle, which could have been the Enclosure and not the actual summit," Mr. Owen said. "The common opinion here in Wyoming and Idaho at that time, and even the opinion of Beaver Dick Leigh, who was a guide for the Hayden Surveys, was that they got so close to the top that it didn't matter. When I couldn't climb to the top from the Upper Saddle, and since their description of a snow slope or ice slope that they went up at that time did not match the scenery when I went up there, I was doubly suspicious about their claim."

Mr. Owen said Langford and Stevenson had reason to say they had reached the top. They thought this would help persuade Congress to give the U.S. Geological and Geographic Survey the money and the authority to explore the West instead of leaving that job to the army.

"Did they get to the top?" Ralph asked.

"Only God will ever know the truth," Mr. Owen said. "In my humble opinion, they did not get to the top, but they had every reason to say they did."

Mr. Owen told us that there have been controversies before as to who reached the top of mountains, but in the mountaineering fraternity it is an unwritten law that if a climber reaches the top of an unscaled peak, it is customary to put up a cairn or leave his name in a bottle or do something to prove to the next party he's been there.

"If you're familiar with mountaineering lore, you'd want to be sure you'd left something up there to prove you'd been to the top," Mr. Owen said. "Because out here in the early exploration days it was common for trappers to brag or say they'd been someplace they hadn't, or stretch the truth a great deal."

We have that phenomenon even today when fish get bigger every month after they're caught. In the early days, we used to say, when we heard these tales, that we had to make allowance for Kentucky windage. A lot of people didn't believe the early trappers when they talked about Yellowstone Park. There was a place there where the water squirted up out of the ground one hundred or so feet in a big burst of steam. But it didn't shoot all the way above the clouds, which may have been one thousand feet high. There were places in Yellowstone where the early trappers could feel warm rock under a cold-water stream, but it wasn't putting blisters on their feet. So the exaggeration of the pioneer trapper Jim Bridger and others led to the opinion of people in the East that reports of Yellowstone Park were tall tales.

We weren't the first young adventurers to benefit from Mr. Owen's experience. He told us about three college students — David DeLap, Andy DePirro, and Quin Blackburn — who had climbed the mountain the year before on August 25. They had corresponded with Mr. Owen, who was living in Los Angeles, and he had explained his route to them. He told them, as he was telling us now, that the key to getting up the Grand Teton was something called the Crawl. One of Mr. Owen's strongest contentions with Langford's account was his failing to mention the Crawl. No one climbing the mountain by that route could overlook this spectacular place.

It was getting toward lunchtime, and Mr. Owen said, "You fellas should just as well have lunch with me. Mrs. Crabtree has some very tempting lunches, and I think you must be getting hungry. We have to get you fattened up for this trip. You still set on going?"

"We sure are. We're going to go."

"Well, I can get Newell Haines to drive you. He drives me around here some whenever I want a car, and I can get him to bring you up to the foot of the mountains," Mr. Owen said. "Geraldine Lucas lives up there alone, and you can meet her and start out from her place. When would you like to go?"

"As soon as possible."

"Well, how about the day after tomorrow?"

"That will be fine. That will give us time to get ready."

"Okay. I'll contact Haines this afternoon and I'll let you know. I think we should leave here early in the morning."

We went back to the Crabtree Hotel and joined the locals and some of the dudes. As we were eating lunch with Mr. Owen, some of the other diners glanced at us and talked among themselves. Two or three of them came over and said, "Are you the boys who think you're going to climb the Grand Teton?"

We said yes. Now, not only were we full-time expedition-eers, we were also celebrities, and I think we rather welcomed our notoriety. As we were walking back to the Kellys' that afternoon, Ralph looked at me and said smilingly, "We're already famous and we haven't even started to climb the Grand Teton yet."

When we got to the Kellys' we told them about our conversation with Mr. Owen. We told them we were capable and had enough experience to climb the same route Mr. Owen and the college students had followed. The Kellys weren't too happy about the situation but they did not object.

Mr. Kelly asked us about our equipment and said that they could loan us a frying pan. He also volunteered to give us a pocketknife when he found out we did not have one. With that taken care of, all we had left to think about was what kind of food to buy for a day or two up on the Grand Teton.

That night we were so excited that it took us a long time to go to sleep on our hay mattresses in George Kelly's barn. We talked about our almost-empty pockets and the limited amount of provisions we would be able to purchase. We were concerned that we had only read about big mountains but we had never climbed any. We wondered what we might encounter on the Grand Teton. Would it be more difficult than the cliffs and chimneys I had climbed around Pillar Falls? If we couldn't do the climb, we could always turn back — at least we thought we could always turn back.

The entire next day we spent planning our expedition. We pictured ourselves as Scott going to the South Pole or Whymper trying to make his first ascent of the Matterhorn. We had matured during the night and considered ourselves adults.

We visited the drugstore and bought a roll of film for Ralph's old box camera. Mr. Porter, the druggist, had heard about our expedition. He figured if we got to the top of the Grand Teton we'd probably use up more than one roll of film, so he gave us another one on the house. Later, when we told George Kelly about Mr. Porter's generosity, he looked at us in disbelief. "That's a little unusual for Porter," he said. "He don't give away many films or anything else."

Then we went to Mercill's store to purchase some food. We looked at the shelves of food, thought about what we could carry, and what we could afford, and decided on some cans of pork and beans, and cans of sardines. We also bought some crackers to eat with our sardines and a few candy bars.

When we went to pay our bill with our meager supply of money, Mrs. Eynon, who was the clerk waiting on us, brought over a few more candy bars and added them to our pile for free. She was worried about us, but also interested in our undertaking and did not discourage us. She said she didn't know why we were going and couldn't understand why people climbed mountains.

Pretty soon, Billy Mercill himself came over to wish us well. He brought with him a couple more candy bars, which he added to our pile. He used an expression that we would hear again and again, "I ain't lost nothin' up there," but, he added, all his life he had looked at those mountains, wondering what it would be like to climb them. He told us, frankly, he wished he were going along with us. We saw in his eyes the wish for adventure, and he seemed to feel sorry that he had never done it himself.

We walked around the square and dropped in at the saloon, where there was a perennial poker game. Everyone talked to us and asked us why we were going up there, repeating again and again, "By God, I ain't lost nothin' up there." One cowboy said, "When they get a trail up there, I'll ride my good horse Baldy up to the top. But until then they can take that mountain and shove it."

The attitude was, as it always had been, that they didn't know why people would be silly enough to climb mountains. We did not defend ourselves when these types of remarks were made. There was no defense, because we too had been raised with the belief that there was something wrong with anyone who would want to climb a mountain.

Why would anyone go anywhere when all there was to bring back was a pebble or a little thin air? When we went into the woods in those days, we were there to fish, hunt, trap, or gather wood. It was acceptable for us to bring back some pretty stones or petrified wood, but people couldn't waste their time climbing mountains. They had to be productive and do something worthwhile when they spent time in the outdoors.

Most of the questions to us were friendly, but some people spoke in a disapproving manner. One of them bluntly said that he thought the sheriff should put us in jail and send us home before we killed ourselves. Others said such an undertaking was silly, especially for young people like us, that we didn't belong up there and we shouldn't be allowed to go. They wondered who was going up after the bodies if we didn't come back. They might go up quite a ways to shoot a mountain sheep with big horns, but there wouldn't be anyone in town who would be very excited about going up and hunting for us.

We took all of this notoriety in good spirits. We were actually flattered to be the center of attention in Jackson. We were celebrities, although I don't think in those days we had ever heard that expression or that word. In the afternoon, we went by Mr. Owen's, where he confirmed our ride to Geraldine Lucas's ranch and told us more about his route.

"Haines will be by here ready to go at eight o'clock in the morning," he said. "If you boys will come down here at about seven, we'll go over to Mrs. Crabtree's and have a good meal before we motor up to the Tetons."

Sleep was hard to come by that night. George Kelly woke us early the next morning. We wrapped our sardines and our pork and beans and our candy bars inside of our patchwork quilts and rolled them up. By putting them diagonally over our shoulders and fastening them together on the bottom with a piece of binding twine we made horseshoes out of the quilts. Those were our packs. It was a customary and practical way of carrying gear and light bedding in those days.

We also had an extra blanket to put into the roll, because the day before as we were leaving Mercill's, Mrs. Eynon appeared with a blanket that she wanted to loan us. She thought we'd be cold way up there on the mountain, where it was sure to be much cooler than in the valley. We accepted her loan, but didn't plan on needing the extra protection.

Before long we were with Mr. Owen in Newell Haines's car, crossing Flat Creek on a rattling plank bridge. The Tetons were in full view with the glaciers and snowfields reflecting the early morning sun. Mr. Owen asked the driver to stop, and we all got out to water the sagebrush and take a detailed look at the mountain.

Ralph and I were silent, almost in shock. We knew the Tetons were high and steep, but we didn't know they were that high and that steep. We had to raise our chins in order to get a look at the summit.

Mr. Owen seemed as excited looking at the mountains as we were. "There's very few mountains in the world that were built like these," he said. "They're caused by a big fault. That's why they don't have any foothills. Most mountains were formed by big humps that come up in the earth and then were gouged out by the glaciers. That's the way the Wind Rivers were created.

"But here you got this fault that forced these mountains straight up seven thousand feet without a single foothill. That's why they're so stunning. That's why Theodore Roosevelt, when he saw them, after he had been all over the world, is reported to have said, 'These are the first mountains I've ever seen that look like mountains should look;'"

Mr. Owen pointed to a big snowfield facing us just under the top of the Grand Teton on the southeast side. He said it was called the Roof. Then he pointed to a smaller permanent snowfield just below the Roof. "It looks like it has legs sticking out from it, and if you have some imagination it looks like an otter. That's why I call it the Otter's Body," he said. "I got right up underneath there one time but was forced to turn back, because in order to get there I had to cross under a waterfall and I got cold and wet. It looks like from there a person could go over that snow and have a fairly easy climb to the top, but nobody's ever tried it."

Some years later I was to go under that same waterfall with Bill Loomis, a prominent member of the American Alpine Club, who was impressed enough by my climbing ability to donate my share of the money needed to go on the first all-American expedition to K2 in the Himalayas in 1938.

"You can't see the place," Mr. Owen said, "where we climbed the last few hundred feet of the Grand Teton, but I can point out how we made our way up to that spot." Ralph and I listened intently as he described the first stages of his ascent.

"Why didn't somebody find the peak between 1898 and 1923?" Ralph asked after a while.

"Well, you know we had a war then," said Mr. Owen. "Many of the young men who might have been interested in climbing were away at the war. And you'll find out if you read the literature of mountaineering that none of the natives in the world that lived close to mountains wanted to climb them. They think it's a little foolish. Although I think they respect and admire me, they don't know why I wanted to climb the mountain in the first place."

Mr. Owen was a wealth of information for us. "You see that black streak just up to the north at the upper part of that saddle? Some people looking at that streak from the valley think it's four or five feet wide. It's actually about forty or fifty feet wide, maybe more. Most people can't judge what's up there. They don't know the size of things as they look at them from this standpoint. I've been around people who thought they saw a man up there on the snowfield, and it was probably a pile of rocks thirty or forty feet high. Judging distance is even harder in the clear air and early sunshine like we have this morning."

We jumped back in the car and sped along toward a black island of timber in the middle of the farms in the sagebrush. "That's Black Tail Butte," Mr. Owen said. "It's about nine miles straight as the crow flies from the top of that butte to the top of the Grand. That's one landmark you can use when you look down from the mountain and judge distance."

The winding road through the sagebrush was abruptly halted by the Snake River. On the other side of the fast stream were a ferry and some cabins. The cabins were home to the Menor brothers, who operated the ferry. Haines got out of the car and yoo-hooed loudly three times. Bill Menor came out of one of the cabins, waved, and shouted, "I'll be right over!"

He boarded the ferry that was attached to a cable stretching across the river. Carried by the current, the boat quickly reached our shore. We drove onto the ferry and soon we had crossed the fast-moving waters of the Snake.

Before we drove off, Mr. Owen said, "We're taking these boys up to see Geraldine Lucas and then they're going on up to try and climb the Grand Teton."

"Well, good luck, fellas, but I ain't lost nothin' up there," Mr. Menor said. It seemed that no one in Jackson's Hole had lost anything up on top of the Grand Teton. I noticed that Mr. Menor seemed a little bit startled when we said we were going to see Geraldine Lucas. Later as we were driving north along the Snake River, Mr. Owen said that perhaps Bill Menor and Geraldine didn't get along.

"Geraldine is very choosy about her friends. She lives up there alone in this beautiful log house winter and summer. She doesn't like dudes to come visit her unless they're specifically invited."

As we went further along the river, the Tetons again broke through the surrounding cottonwoods. They were much closer now, and we had to raise our chins higher to see the top. Soon we reached Cottonwood Creek, where we rumbled across another plank bridge. On the other side was Geraldine Lucas's house.

She came out looking quite stern until she recognized Mr. Owen. "What are you people up to now?" she asked.

"These boys are going to climb the Grand Teton, or think they are at least," Mr. Owen said. "Perhaps when they come down or if they have any trouble they could stop here on their way back."

"You're going to climb the Grand Teton?" she asked.

"Well, we're sure going to try," I said.

"I've dreamed of doing that myself," she said. "Maybe if you get up there, I can make it too." She assured us that we would be welcome on our return trip.

Now we really had to raise our chins to see the top. We were anxious to get away, so with many good wishes and good-byes we loaded our horseshoe-shaped quilt packs over our shoulders and started off across the sagebrush flat.

We followed the route Geraldine had suggested for reaching the canyon that led to the Lower Saddle and Mr. Owen's route up the Grand Teton. "Probably the best way to go is to head over there to your left a little bit and hit Burnt Wagon Gulch," Geraldine had told us. "I've never been up beyond there, but that will lead you into the canyon."

After we'd gone a couple of hundred yards, we looked back and Mr. Owen and Geraldine were still watching us. It was an ideal day. The sagebrush was pungent, and I was reminded of *Riders of the Purple Sage*, a Zane Grey book I had read recently. Flowers were blooming everywhere, and we did not know their names. There were bird sounds all around us, and in the sky two huge birds with white heads were soaring. "Them's eagles," Ralph said.

II

Soon we were out of the sage and into the timber, where we had to dodge swamps created by beaver that had built up dams on the smaller streams coming off the mountains. Instead of cutting south to hit what Geraldine had called Burnt Wagon Gulch, we took to a ridge where there was less brush and we could make better progress.

As we went higher and higher with great speed and without stopping, we looked south toward the canyon that was supposed to take us to the saddle. The traverse was over steep grassy slopes and rock outcroppings. I don't know why, but we silently chose to try the East Ridge instead of the Owen Route. We drifted north where we saw a U-shaped valley of smooth rock still polished from the glacier that ran down it thousands of years ago. In the numerous cracks and ledges of these rocks a few scrub pines grew, and flowers bloomed from small patches of soil that clung to the rock.

We ran up through the ledges of the smooth rocks. Soon we reached a lake right at the bottom of the East Ridge. We stopped there and had a couple of cans of sardines. Of course, we threw the empty cans into the flowers. No one in those days would have done any differently.

Comfortable marmots waddled toward the safety of their dens as we approached. We saw the coneys running around bringing out mouthfuls of grass and flowers to put on top of the flat rocks. Ralph told me about the coneys' lifestyle.

"They pick out the kinds of things they want to eat in the wintertime," Ralph said. "They put them out on the rocks and let them cure just like you let your hay cure before you stack it in the barn. If you have too much moisture in it, it will spoil. That's why they let it dry just to the perfect state where it's still green and tasty but not wet enough to spoil. When it's just right they bring it back underneath the rocks and store it."

"What happens if it rains?" I asked. "Sometimes after it rains our hay spoils before we can get it dried out on the ground."

"Well, they're too smart for that," Ralph said. "Before it starts to rain they go out and gather up what's on the rocks and take it back under the rocks until the sun comes out again. Then they bring it back out and let it cure some more."

Between the lake and the mountain was a small flat field of flowers and small pines. Beyond that were boulders, some bigger than houses, that guarded the way to the East Ridge. A stream running down from the glacier under the North Face of the Grand Teton had built up a delta in the lake. We called it Delta Lake and that's what it's called today.

It was warm. There was no breeze. White clouds drifted in slow motion high above the Grand Teton. We threw down our blankets and food and also our denim jackets. We took off our shirts and wrapped them around our waists, leaving us with only our bib-top overalls, our socks, and our cowboy-type boots to protect us from the elements. Taking off almost at a run with only a lasso rope for equipment, we headed for the peak.

We wound around and over cabin-sized boulders until we came to a short pitch that took some scrambling. When I got to the top of the pitch I threw down the rope for Ralph. Above that we scrambled for several hundred feet more until we hit the first pinnacle on the East Ridge of the Grand Teton.

There we suddenly found ourselves in a different realm of mountaineering. On the east side it went straight up and was unclimbable. We tried to skirt this pinnacle on the north side, but we got into some loose boulders, many of which rolled down and bounced over the cliff with a touch of the hand. A thousand feet below we heard them boom as they hit the edge of the glacier. Deciding it was too dangerous, we turned around, went down a bit, and skirted the pinnacle to the south. We found a niche that went around the pinnacle. It was difficult climbing, far more difficult than we had expected.

The niche ran into a little gully full of snow. We kicked steps up a ways to where a huge rock jammed into the gully and temporarily blocked us from reaching the East Ridge again. After scrambling around it, we saw that we could continue. Suddenly, we realized it was evening.

We had to decide what to do. There was no use to continue and to get into the more difficult climbing during the night. Back where we had gone through the crack on the south side of the ridge there was some protection. We decided to spend the night there and run on up to the top the next morning. We backtracked to the protected lee and, in the evening warmth, watched the shadows of the Tetons blanket the valley. They crept across Jackson's Hole until they lost themselves in the horizon above the Wind Rivers.

Before dark we were sound asleep. We were awakened by a terrific boom. Over toward Pierre's Hole, which is a valley like Jackson's Hole but on the west side of the mountains, huge black clouds were rolling in, spitting lightning down toward the peaks. Soon there was a continuous rumbling, and the echoes pounded back and forth between the walls of the Tetons. "It sounds like a symphony," Ralph said. We were frightened, but we did not know the terror that awaited us.

Suddenly, the wind started. It blew sixty or seventy miles an hour and roared around the corners of the pinnacles. Then the rain came. It didn't start with just sprinkles; it started like someone was pouring water out of a bucket. We were drenched and we saw streams coming off the mountain and leaping into nothingness.

Almost as abruptly as they had started, the rain and lightning stopped. The howling wind that announced the beginning of the storm ceased. But this turned out to be only a short reprieve. Snowflakes began to fall through the cold darkness. Our shelter was about three feet wide and allowed some protection if we huddled against the north wall of what now had become a torture chamber. We tried to keep warm by exercising as much as our narrow space would allow. Soon we were pressing our bodies together, fighting for what we now thought might be survival.

We were in shock over the unexpected turn of events. "We should have brung our coats," I chattered to Ralph.

"Damn poor judgment," Ralph said. The word judgment was not used very often by my family. They talked about it by another name; it was called horse sense. Some people had horse sense and some people didn't. If a person was going to get along and do things right and be able to look ahead and see what was coming, he had to have horse sense.

"We have no horse sense," I said. Since we had no watch either we didn't know how long we had dozed before we were awakened by the storm. Time passed slowly, slowly, slowly. I wondered about the temperature. The wet rocks were now glazed with a slick coating of ice on which the snow continued to pile up.

I thought about my coat and imagined lying on my quilt in the warm sun we had enjoyed at noon. Sitting on a rock near the edge of the lake, eating our sardines, the world was so beautiful, our hopes were so high, our ambition unobstructed. How could the world change so suddenly?

Now we were really suffering. I thought of a story I had read about prisoners being tortured. I thought, perhaps this isn't so bad — if we live through it. We kept looking toward the east for the first glimmer of light. Only hours earlier, we had looked to that direction from our heights and had a clear view of Jackson's Hole. We had seen the Snake River cutting through that settled valley. Far to the east and a little south were the snowcapped Wind River Mountains. Winding through the sagebrush past timbered islands and across Cottonwood Creek was the road to Geraldine's house. We had even seen an automobile, like a speck, sitting at the end of the road.

Now darkness had erased all that, and all we saw was snow and ice. We were numb from the cold. The night was an eternity. Finally, a slight glow of light came out of the eastern sky. We tried to wait patiently until the sun peeked over the Gros Ventre

Range. The clouds were visible now, milling all around us and letting the sun through as they parted. As the sky brightened, however, we saw that the trouble from the storm had just begun.

We could not retreat down the mountain. The difficult climbing we had come up just below our shelter was slicked over by ice and covered by three or four inches of snow. No secure holds were available to us on this steep slope down to where we would have had a fairly easy scramble to our camp at Delta Lake.

Turning to the west, we surveyed the gully that led up to the big chockstone we had visited the evening before. Looking down that gully, it seemed that we could reach a platform some distance below, but clouds obscured what lay below the platform. In our desperation, we thought we might escape the mountain that way.

Our minds were not working well. We moved slowly, like the rattlesnakes I used to find early in the morning under the irrigation canvases on our farm near Twin Falls. As we neared the platform we discovered a narrow section filled with ice from the runoff the previous evening. It wasn't very far down, and the platform looked comfortable, so we slid down this icy chute. The clouds still hid the space below the platform. I picked up a large rock and tossed it over the side into the clouds. We waited and waited and then we heard it hit. I think our horse sense was starting to get better. We knew we could not climb down there nor could we jump into the featherbed-looking clouds below. There was nothing to do but to go back up to our crevice.

But when we turned around we found our retreat was cut off. What meager handholds we could find were covered with ice. The chute looked impossible to climb. I thought about the mice we used to catch in our barn by putting milk in the bottom of a bucket. We would prop up a stick against the edge of the bucket. The mice would climb the stick and jump down into the bucket to get food. When they were full and wanted to leave they could not get back out because there were no holds for their claws. This was the way we rid our barn of mice, and I thought this might be the way the Grand Teton would rid itself of us.

III

We thought we were finished. We were forced to admit the reality of our dire situation. Thinking we were goners, we whimpered a bit. But I had read many Zane Grey books and the heroes always faced terrible odds but never gave up. If we were going to die, we had to die fighting.

Then we remembered the knife that Mr. Kelly had loaned us. It had a solid blade about three or four inches long. I pulled it out of my pocket, opened it up, and started to chisel a handhold in the ice. It took a long time. Then I chiseled footholds in the ice and then another handhold. I now had two feet and two hands in notches I had made. With one hand I could reach up and chisel other little notches where I could put my hands and feet higher up the wall. One hour later we were up the twelve-foot ice wall to where we could climb back to our all-night home.

Just then the miracle happened that saved our lives. The clouds parted and we were bathed in full, warming sun. Our hands and feet tingled and stung with the new warmth. Suddenly we felt alive. We had hope. We thought that we could live. I sometimes think now that the only reason we survived was because we did not know we were supposed to die. Perhaps hypothermia was in the dictionary at that time, but we had never heard of it.

Soon the snow started to melt, and little rivulets of water ran down over the cliffs. Sparrows, now known as rosy finches, were jumping around on the snow looking for bugs that had died during the storm. Soon the pain had left our hands and feet, and we were filled again with optimism. At least our horse sense had grown enough to know that we did not want to go on up the mountain now. We had to try to get back to the safety and comfort of our camp at Delta Lake.

We waited in the warmth until noon to let the ice and snow on the rocks below melt. Ralph went down the steep cliff tied on to the rope that I held above. Then I tied the end of the rope around me and Ralph held it in back of some rocks as I carefully climbed down to his side.

From there it was freewheeling. We scrambled down the easy slope to the cliff that separated us from the boulder field below. This seemed easy to us now. We practically ran to our camp, which was warm again. We heard the whistle of marmots and saw the coneys bringing their grass out onto the rocks.

We laid out our quilts and sat in the warm sunshine. Now that we were warm we realized how hungry we were. We gulped down most of our sardines and pork and beans. Then we lay down in the sun and slept. We woke late the next morning overheated, since we had gone to sleep with our treasured jackets on and fully buttoned. We ate some more pork and beans and finished off with a candy bar given to us by Billy Mercill. Then we started to talk about going back to Jackson.

"I don't want to go back to Jackson and face those cowboys," Ralph said.

"I don't either," I replied.

"I know they ain't lost nothin' up there in that crack where we spent the night," he said.

"Me neither," I replied. We both laughed. Humor and life and hope and ambition had returned to our previously frozen bodies. But we had left Jackson with newfound recognition and we didn't want to go back to be laughed at. We were important and somewhat admired by people like Billy Mercill and Geraldine Lucas, and we weren't ready to give up that admiration.

"We could sure get up those long snow slopes that go around under where we spent the night," I said. "That's where Mr. Owen says the black streak runs, and it goes through the upper part of the Lower Saddle. Maybe we can get to his route that way. I don't want any more of the East Ridge."

"We'll take along our jackets," Ralph said, "and the moment we see a black cloud we'll come down fast."

"I never knew weather could change that fast and that furious," I said.

That afternoon we planned the next leg of our expedition for early the next morning. We took out George Kelly's pocketknife, cut down some young pine trees, stripped off the bark and limbs, and made imitation alpenstocks out of them. Next, we took the trusty pocketknife and cut down a few larger pine trees that were three or four inches thick on the bottom. I'd learned to cut down trees this size with a pocketknife in less than a minute. Then we cut off the pine boughs and made beautiful pine-bough beds. As a scout in Twin Falls, I had received a badge for being an expert pine-bough bed maker.

That evening, watching the shadow of the Grand Teton creep across Jackson's Hole, we ate the last of our food and tucked ourselves into our bedding on top of the pine-bough beds. Before we fell asleep we talked about the cold night we had spent on the mountain. I quoted a line from Robert Service: "Talk of your cold through the parka's fold, it stung like the driven nail."

Ralph countered with some more ancient stuff that I had never heard before. "The hare limped through the frozen grass. The owl for all his feathers was acold."

To which I replied, "A chill no coat however stout,/ Of homespun stuff could quite shut out,/ A hard, dull bitterness of cold,/ The coming of the snow-storm told."

Our common bone, the one we both shared, was a poem called "The Wanderlust," by Robert Service. I think we both imagined that we were out on a great adventure in a world we were just discovering.

"Oh, I'll beat it once more in the morning, boys,
With a pinch of tea and a crust;
For it's so-long to all
When you answer the call of the Wan-der-lust."

We fell asleep dreaming of our adventure to come. When we woke, the sun was just peeping over the Gros Ventres. Putting our blankets under a boulder for protection, we grabbed our alpenstocks and started for the summit. We crossed over to the foot of the big snow slope that borders the south part of the Grand Teton and started up, kicking steps in the semifrozen snow. It was tedious and time-consuming but a fairly easy part of the ascent. At one time we heard some rocks coming from above, where we had spent the night. They leaped through the air down to our snowfield, hitting with a thud and burying themselves in the snow.

"Be too bad if one of them hits us," Ralph said.

"If we see 'em comin', we can dodge them," I said, recalling my baseball experience in the batter's box. We came over the ridge at the top of the snow slope and found ourselves on a small glacier, which we crossed with ease. A second steeper snowfield proved more difficult to traverse. We had to use our alpenstocks for balance in the soft snow. Ahead lay a band of charcoal-colored rocks.

The black streak was just as Mr. Owen had described it. We followed it to the upper part of the Lower Saddle. There we were greeted by a terrific new view. To the west, over Pierre's Hole, we could see the outline of the Sawtooth Range in the distance and the point where we had come around the mountains on our way to Jackson — the spot where we saw the Grand Teton for the first time. Looking south, the mountain dropped away from us, flattened out, and rose up again to form the steep north side of the Middle Teton. It looked like a giant could straddle this saddle in comfort. All such spaces between nearby peaks are generally called saddles.

We were comforted by the knowledge that we were now on the Owen Route and we had a detailed description of that route all the way to the top of the Grand Teton. We scrambled toward the Upper Saddle between the Grand Teton itself and a prominent pinnacle to the west. Most of our climbing continued to be up snowfields, and where climbable snow did not exist we had to clamber over small rocky cliffs. Sometimes we were forced onto a little ridge that separated our gully from a deeper gully that ran along the vertical west wall, below the Upper Saddle.

As we arrived at the Upper Saddle we could see what Mr. Owen called the Enclosure. We decided to investigate the mysterious stone structure that topped the pinnacle to the west. It took about ten minutes to reach it. The rocks undoubtedly had been set up by some force other than nature. Several thin slabs formed a circle a couple feet high with a flat bottom of debris and dust crumbling off the surrounding rocks. It would have taken a great deal of energy and some time for its builder to have moved the stones around as we found them. The structure would not have offered a great deal of protection against a strong west wind.

One could only wonder whether it had been built by some native or by some early trapper who had strayed up there.

It seemed to serve no purpose except, we imagined, as a lookout for Indians who, from that vantage point, could see Pierre's Hole and perhaps see the dust rising from approaching horsemen in the distance. However, it would have been difficult to get to. Later, Mr. Owen told me that a trapper by the name of Michaud had tried to climb the Grand Teton in the early days and that some people thought maybe he had built the Enclosure.

We were shocked when we looked at the West Face of the Grand Teton across the narrow saddle that separated us from the main peak. It dropped straight down into an awful chasm of snow and ice two or three thousand feet below. It was a view that made me shrink back from the edge. Straight across the Upper Saddle, the vertical West Face ended with what looked like an unclimbable wall.

The wall was imposing, but we knew its secret. Thrilled with the chance to reach the actual summit of the Grand Teton, we rushed down the slopes from the Enclosure and crossed the narrow saddle over to the base of the wall. Again we examined the wall. Certainly we could not climb it. Lying on the ground was a pile of iron spikes. Ralph picked one up and inspected it. It had a hole in one end through which a rope could be threaded. The other end was pointed. These evidently were the spikes left by the Owen party twenty-six years before.

No one seeing the Grand Teton from the Enclosure would have dreamed there was a passage around to the north where the rock was actually overhanging. However, below the overhang, which was like a bulge in the mountain, there was a sharp edge that could be grabbed. I took ahold of this edge and worked my way around the rounded corner, using only my hands with my belly pressed up against the rock. Halfway around I realized I wasn't using the proper technique. My neophyte friends at Twin Falls were rock huggers. On their first climbs, they would keep their bodies close to the rock to feel safe, when actually they should have raised up their hind ends away from the rock so their feet would be against footholds at a more direct angle. This pressure against the rocks would keep their feet from slipping.

For a moment I was a neophyte myself and rolled my belly over the rocks. Several years later, when I took Glenn Exum, one of my first guides, up the Grand Teton he dubbed this place the Belly Roll, and the Belly Roll it remains today. As I moved along the Belly Roll I could not see what was on the other side, but I could look down thousands of feet to the tops of the pine trees below. It isn't a place for people with acrophobia. I stretched my leg around the corner and found a place to stand. This enabled me to swing around to the small platform that Mr. Owen had told us was there. On the platform, I could stand up straight underneath the overhang.

I yelled for Ralph to come on and as he swung his leg over to where I stood, I guided his foot to the firm foothold I had found. From there the ledge continued under the overhang for about thirty feet. Because the ledge was only a little wider than a person's body, we knew if we tried to crawl across it we would be pushed out by the overhang. So we squirmed our way along the ledge, one behind the other. We now understood why Mr. Owen called this spot the "cooning" place, referring to a raccoon and how it climbs and squirms its way through small holes and openings.

On the other side of the ledge was a place with barely enough room for us to stand, the awful space still below us. Above our heads was a chimney slanting up at a comfortable angle that seemed plenty large to climb. My only concern was its slick walls. There was a little chockstone securely wedged in the bottom of this chimney, and it was evident from the debris around it that it had been there for years, perhaps centuries.

First I tried to loop our rope around the chockstone, but the rock slanted downward and was too slick to hold it. Then Ralph and I tied on at each end of the rope. He boosted me up high enough to take ahold of the chockstone with questionable grip. From there I found a good handhold in back of the rock. Chinning myself up, I was able to wiggle into a stable position. By putting one hand on one side of the chimney and one on the other, I climbed to the top, where I got behind another crack and was safe from every side. I brought up the rope as Ralph climbed, and he used it to help him get over the chockstone.

We scrambled with care up over a series of chimneys, rock slabs, and broken ledges straight toward what looked like the top from the Enclosure. To get there, we had to pass around on the south side and then climb from the east. From there we could look down to where we had spent our terrible night.

From the Enclosure we had seen the bare knob that looked like the summit of the Grand Teton. Now that we were on that knob we could see, as Mr. Owen had told us, that the real summit was actually about 250 feet to the north and much higher. It was an easy walk for us through the snow to get there.

At two o'clock we stood on top of the Grand Teton. We were silent for a long time. Eventually, we became conscious of ourselves and hugged each other. We raised our hands and yelled as loud as we could, hoping that the people of Jackson heard us. Maybe some of the "ain't lost nothin' up there" people wished they were up here with us. It was the biggest and most thrilling moment of my life.

In the direction of Yellowstone, we saw smoke rising, perhaps from a small forest fire. We wrote our names on a piece of paper and put them in the bottle that contained the names of the 1898 Owen party and the two parties that had climbed the Grand the year before. We counted the number of times the edges of the Rocky Mountain Club banner that Owen's party had left on top was burnt, presumably from being hit by lightning.

We got out our old box camera. It took good pictures. Later, we had them developed at Porter's drugstore, and the next year he was selling them as postcards, especially the one of the Rocky Mountain Club pennant bitten by lightning. When I mentioned to him that we had not given him the right to sell our pictures just because he had developed them, he handed me a five-dollar bill to clear his conscience. It was probably more than he ever made from selling the pictures.

The bright sun, angling downward toward the Sawtooths in the distance, brought us back down to earth. We suddenly realized how late it was getting and that we must get off the top.

"I never want to spend another night like the other night as long as I live," Ralph said, and I didn't either. I wasn't going to spend one more night bivouacked on the mountain if I could help it. Before leaving, Ralph posed dramatically with his hands around his mouth and yelled down to a speck of a cabin near Cottonwood Creek, more than six thousand feet below us. "We made it, Geraldine," he yelled. "Tell Billy Owen we made it."

Then we hurried off the peak. When we got to the chimney that was blocked by the chockstone, I tied a rope around Ralph and belayed him from my secure place. He dropped down to the ledge below and yelled for me to come on. Holding on to the top of the chockstone, I dangled my feet over the edge. He took ahold of them and guided me to the ground. The "cooning" place and the Belly Roll were not as frightening the second time around, and we were quickly past them. We rushed down the mountain as fast as safety allowed.

Despite having eaten our last food the evening before, we were still full of energy and enthusiasm. Our boots were fast deteriorating from scrambling over the rocks and through the wet snow.

When we got past the black streak we had to make a decision. The sun was getting lower and a cool wind was blowing in. The snow, which the morning sunshine had softened, was starting to harden and refreeze. "By the time we get to the steep snow leading down to the glacier and then the long snowfield going down to our camp, it's all going to be like ice and we won't be able to get down safely," I said.

Ralph agreed. "Let's escape by Mr. Owen's route," he said. "We'll go down the canyon the way he came up and if we don't make it back to camp, we'll at least be in the timber where we can build a fire. It doesn't look like there's going to be a storm tonight."

Keeping our eyes out for the Owen Route, we scrambled down to the bottom part of the Lower Saddle. We had to climb down a steep pitch of rock to get onto a moraine of the glacier that hung on the northeast side of the Middle Teton. The moraine, which gave us a good gravelly path, led us to some level snow on the lower part of that glacier. From there, we raced further down the valley as darkness fell.

A high ridge was all that separated us from our pine-bough beds on the shores of Delta Lake. There looked to be some climbable terrain alongside a stream that flowed down from the ridge. That is the route we took, after stopping to drink some cool water to extinguish our thirst.

"I'm kind of hungry," Ralph said. It was now twenty-four hours since we had eaten a morsel of food.

"I'm not kind of hungry," I said. "I could eat raw chitlins."

Ralph was leading the way when we reached the top of the stream as it disappeared over a cliff. Poking our heads over the ridge, we were startled to find a beautiful lake. It was such a surprise, we named it Surprise Lake. It remains Surprise Lake today. We didn't realize then that there were already many Surprise Lakes around the country.

At this point we were traveling by twilight. I cannot remember to this day the details of how we got down the other side of that cliff to Delta Lake, but we made it somehow. It was dark and late when we reached the security of our blankets. Almost immediately, without thought of the morrow or the future, we flopped down on our soft beds.

It seemed only a moment later that I awoke with the sun in my face and heard the jays and the whistle of the marmots again. My movement awakened Ralph, and as he sat up and rubbed his eyes he said, "Another beautiful day."

"Yeah," I said. "But what are we going to do?"

But Ralph was not ready to face reality yet. "That rain the other night while we were in the crack has made the flowers grow bigger and there's even more of them, new kinds that weren't bloomin' when we went up the mountain," Ralph said. He had gathered all the varieties he could find the day we spent at the camp after our horrible bivouac. He was anxious to remember them and to learn their names. It was no accident that this brilliant young man knew so much.

I had gotten acquainted with Ralph when I was the leading man in a play he wrote and produced for a women's club in Twin Falls. I wasn't much of an actor, but Ralph told me I did a great job. The play was called *Ashes of Jazz*. Ralph had written other plays too. He convinced women's clubs around the country that his plays were moneymakers and had the newspaper clippings to prove it. If people weren't sold enough on Ralph's plays, he would sell them on the idea of making their children promising young actors and actresses. This usually worked.

But this morning I was not interested in admiring the wildflowers or thinking about amateur theater. We were broke. We had not eaten in thirty-six hours. The soles were coming off our shoes, and something had to be done with them before we could walk down to the valley. How were we going to get back to Jackson? Would Geraldine greet us and invite us in for some hot oatmeal, or would she shoo us away as she did some of the other people who came to her place unannounced? If we went out to the road, were there any cars that would come along and pick us up and take us to Jackson? And what would happen then?

"We can stay at the Kellys' a few days longer," Ralph said. "But I don't think we'd be welcome much longer than that."

"I could get a job on a ranch," I said. "All those wooden pens we saw comin' up here were empty and they've gotta be filled up. We didn't see any cows on the way up here. They're all back in the mountains getting fat on your flowers. But in the fall when they come back here they're goin' to need a lot of hay to keep them warm all winter."

"Well, I might get a job in a café," Ralph said. "I can wash dishes and wait tables and even fry a hamburger if I have to. But I suppose when my people hear about the climb, they'll want me to come home for a while."

"How are they gonna hear about it?" I said. "Are you gonna tell 'em?"

"No, I'm not gonna tell 'em. They'll read about it. I'm gonna write something for the *Des Moines Register* and they're gonna print it. They'll hear about it all over Iowa and the Midwest. Everybody will be a little surprised, but they won't be too astonished. They already think I'm sort of funny, writing poetry and putting on plays when I should be out huskin' corn. I think my folks won't mind, even though they don't approve."

Our first order of business was a weekly bath. I was used to taking one every Saturday night on the ranch. Despite the frigid water, we took a dip in Delta Lake. After drying off, we turned our attention to getting off the mountain.

Our biggest problem was how to repair our tattered shoes. "We'll cut up one of the quilts," I said. Using Mr. Kelly's pocketknife, we cut one of the quilts to pieces. We used some for padding our sore feet and the remaining strips to hold our disintegrating soles and unraveled seams together. Loading up the rest of our meager gear we left the lake, using our alpenstock walking sticks.

Soon we were at the foot of the mountains and we wormed our way through the sagebrush over to Geraldine's cabin. We knocked on the door, but she was not home. Her car was not in the garage, so we trudged on without the food we had hoped for, over the plank bridge and down to the road near Timbered Island, an island of pine trees in a sea of sagebrush, the remnants of an old glacier moraine. We sat down on a rock and waited. As we sat there in our pitiful clothing with our feet wrapped in pieces of quilt, Ralph remarked that we looked like George Washington crossing the Delaware. He had seen a picture of that somewhere.

Finally, a car came along. The driver stopped and both he and his wife smiled kindly at us, which was a great relief. Maybe they weren't smiling; maybe they were laughing. "What are you fellas doing out here?" the driver asked.

"We just climbed to the top of the Grand Teton," I said. "And we're lookin' for a ride back to Jackson."

"I guess we can figure that one out," he said. "Why don't you boys jump in back. It's kind of full of our stuff, but I think maybe you can get in."

We squeezed in and the car sped toward Menor's Ferry, leaving the customary plume of dust behind us. We were silent most of the way, but the driver did ask us some questions about our adventure. Although his tone was still friendly, he seemed dubious of our story.

When we got into town, the driver stopped across from Mercill's. As if by magic, our vibes or maybe our odor permeated the town. A crowd gathered around us as soon as we were out of the car. Billy Mercill came out of his store and so did Porter, the druggist. People from the hardware store were there, and we saw people coming out of the saloon, even leaving their poker game to come see the kids who had left a few days before to climb the Grand Teton.

Of course, the first question was "Did you get to the top?" "Sure did," we said. As we kept answering that we got to the top, there were looks back and forth and smiles of disbelief and doubt. Evidently somebody had gone to Mr. Owen's cabin, because we saw him almost running down the street. When he reached us he asked how we did.

"We got to the top," I said. "We made it following your route after trying our own way up the East Ridge."

We reported on the many lightning burns along the edges of the metal Rocky Mountain Club flag from the 1898 expedition. We told Mr. Owen we saw his name chiseled in the rock on top and that we had opened the bottle and found the record of his 1898 climb and the names of the two parties that had climbed the Grand Teton in 1923.

Everybody listened intently, and soon Mr. Owen was convinced. He put his hands dramatically on our shoulders, turned to the crowd, and said with authority, "These young men have been to the very top of the Grand Teton!"

CHAPTER TWO

THE KID GROWS UP

"The ascents of this great peak made last year and the present season by Ralph Herron and Paul Petzoldt, as chronicled in the columns of a recent issue, have revived the interest in Wyoming's noted mountain."
— Jackson Hole Courier, *August 21, 1924*

"It is also interesting to note that Mr. Paul Petzoldt has ascended the peak four times this summer, the only man known to reach the summit of Teton County's peerless peak more than twice."
— Jackson Hole Courier, *September 4, 1924*

About a week after I had taken the first dead man off the Grand Teton, two dudes showed up at the Lucas ranch and said they wanted me to show them the way up the Grand Teton. At that time, I was very happy working for Bill Lucas, Geraldine's brother, where I felt that I was considered one of the family. I was great friends with one of Bill's sons, who was near my age, and he had started to teach me how to ride bucking horses. That was a mistake on my part, because I wasn't as successful in my ambition to become the world's leading bronc rider as I was in becoming a well known mountaineer.

On August 14, 1925, I was sweating profusely when two young men approached the haystack. Instinctively, I recognized that they were dudes. I had seen them around town. They asked to speak to me, so I motioned to the buckrakes to stop. The other workers wanted to get a drink of cold water anyway, so I jumped off the half-made stack to talk to the strangers. They introduced themselves as Mitchell Gratwich and Clement Cobb from New York City and asked me if I would show them the way up the Grand Teton.

Sixteen-year-old Paul Petzoldt ready for a climb, looking more like a Boy Scout than a Teton mountain guide. (Teton County Historical Center)

I told them I wouldn't show them the way up but I would guide them up there, which meant I was in charge of the expedition. I wasn't going to go along just to obey orders and to point the way.

Once that was clear, they asked me how much I would charge. Well, I was making a dollar a day stacking hay, which was common wages then for hayhands, along with room and board, so I decided to start with a fairly high figure. "How about one hundred bucks?" I said, which is what Mr. Owen had paid me when I took him to the top on his sixty-fifth birthday the year before. This shocked them a little, but they said they would talk it over. I crawled back on the haystack and started to stack hay again. After a while they came back and asked me when I could go. I said the next morning would be fine. I asked someone to replace me on the stack so I could discuss the particulars of the trip with Gratwich and Cobb. I had an understanding with the Lucases that I could stop haying if I had a chance to guide.

In three days I was back on a haystack with a summer's wages in my pocket. I had a new racket.

***

I had worked as a guide for three climbs the summer before in 1924. It all really started that morning when Ralph and I arrived back in Jackson after our first ascent. After we told our story to the curious locals, Mrs. Crabtree invited us into the dining room of the Crabtree Hotel and filled our empty stomachs with pancakes until we were stuffed.

Fortune was smiling on us. We had been lucky to meet Mr. Owen, lucky to get off the mountain alive, lucky to get a ride into Jackson. Just before we left the square a rancher had offered Ralph and me a way to stay in town.

"Are you fellas looking for a job?" he asked. "My sister Geraldine told me about you and said you were farmboys. We're going to start haying soon, and I could use some extra help."

"I come from a farm in Iowa," Ralph said, "but I've never done much farm work. I'm an author. I don't know one end of a pitchfork from the other."

"I'm a farmboy," I said. "I've worked with a lot of hay. If you want a good haystacker, I can do that too."

"That's just what I'm lookin' for," he said. "As soon as you want you can come work for me."

"I'll do that right away," I said. "But I'll have to find some other shoes first."

With that, the man reached into his pocket and pulled out a five-dollar bill. "My name is Bill Lucas," he said. "Our ranch is just out of town towards Wilson up Spring Gulch a little ways. Everybody knows where I live. As soon as you're ready to go to work let me know or come on out. I'll be expecting you."

A short while later, as we settled down outside Mr. Owen's cabin, Mr. Owen said, "I've been thinking. Ralph, you say you're going to leave, but Paul, if you go to work for Bill Lucas helping him put up his summer hay supply, you'll be around. I'm thinking that maybe I could get you to take me to the top of the Grand Teton. You're the first people I've talked to that have been up there since my '98 ascent." Mr. Owen wasn't around in the summer of 1923, so he didn't get to meet the two parties that went up the Grand that year.

"Paul, I might hire you, so you wouldn't miss any wages from your work out on Bill Lucas's ranch. I could get Ike Powell to pack us up through Death Canyon over on the west side. I think that would be the easiest way for me to get to the saddle." Mr. Owen said he was going to see Dr. Huff for a thorough examination to see if there would be any risk in climbing the Grand Teton again at his age. "Think about it," he said.

I started work at Bill Lucas's ranch. In a few days, Mr. Owen called and arranged to take me up to Geraldine's place, where I was to stay and do some scouting for him. I explored the area above Bradley Lake and thought I could guide the horses into the canyon where a camp could be made. It would present an easier approach than the horse camp used by Mr. Owen in 1898.

With Ralph's and my ascent, local interest in climbing on the Grand Teton exploded. Suddenly, some locals wanted to join us; many who had always proudly stated that "they ain't lost nothin' up there" were wondering what it would be like to really climb to the top. Mr. Owen was encouraged that I, though only sixteen, would be on hand to show the way.

Geraldine decided to join the party. Mrs. Eugene Amoretti, a beautiful and enthusiastic woman who ran a dude ranch near Jackson Lake that sometimes had the Rockefellers and officials from Yellowstone Park as guests, wanted to come along, especially after hearing that Geraldine was making the climb. She hired Gibb Scott, an energetic packer, to take her to timberline with his horse outfit and to accompany her to the peak.

Frank Peterson, who had become a successful rancher in the valley since climbing the Grand with Mr. Owen in '98, decided to join Mr. Owen and see if these "two old codgers" could do it again.

Jesse Dewey, a member of an adventurous pioneer family from Pierre's Hole, was ecstatic about his invitation to join the party.

Fred Koerner, whose German background instilled in him an interest in mountaineering, along with young Jack Crawford, a guest of Geraldine's, and Mr. Owen's friend Charles Purdy, also joined the group. Miss Yvonne Deloney, a young girl from the well-known Deloney family, went along to accompany Geraldine, with a promise to her family not to climb above timberline.

The party gathered at Geraldine's cabin early on the morning of August 12, 1924. It was not a well-organized expedition, since separate arrangements had been made for packing food and equipment. I ran back and forth guiding the pack outfits and riders through a labyrinth of downed timber and over the steep ledges that led into the bottom of Bradley Canyon. We were near timberline when we stopped at a flat place good for camping, with plenty of vegetation for the horses, cool springs running out of the rocks, and lots of dried wood for campfires. At five o'clock all were there, including Gibb Scott and Mrs. Amoretti, who had gotten a late start but had followed the horse tracks up to the mouth of the canyon to our camp.

Early the next morning the party started for the peak, but before long it disintegrated into a chaotic race to the top at a pace destined to eliminate all but the strongest members. I stayed back with Mr. Owen, trying to get him to slow down. It was no use. Ahead, younger and stronger members scrambled toward the Lower Saddle. Geraldine soon tired, and Mrs. Amoretti became ill with mountain sickness, a common ailment of inexperienced climbers that is caused by the high altitude and the mental and physical stress of climbing.

Mr. Owen kept taking his pulse periodically, and when it reached the rate that Dr. Huff had warned him about he reluctantly gave up. He told me to catch the others and keep them from killing themselves. Gibb Scott, released by the ill Mrs. Amoretti, was also trying to catch the others.

I raced to the head of the party at the Upper Saddle and brought some organization to the climb. Setting up my rope for climbers to use in exposed places, I supervised the dangerous ascent and descent over the "cooning" place and the final six hundred feet to the top. Thus, on August 13, Koerner, Dewey, Crawford, Scott, and I reached the summit. Peterson and Purdy had turned back with Mr. Owen. Although I had reached the top that time, I considered the climb unsuccessful because Mr. Owen hadn't been able to make it.

***

Maybe the only one madder on that climb than Mr. Owen about not being able to reach the summit of the Grand Teton was Geraldine Lucas. Even though she was fifty-nine, she hadn't been stopped by her heart rate, as Mr. Owen had. She was stopped by the disorganization and lack of cooperation of the climbing party.

I had only been back working at her brother's ranch one day after the failed Owen expedition when she drove out to see me and asked me point blank if I would take her to the top of the Grand Teton. "I've heard talk around town that it's no place for a woman and that women should not be allowed up there," she said. "People just don't understand women like myself."

I had been warned by some of the locals that Geraldine was difficult to get along with and hard to understand, but I found her friendly and her great intelligence stimulating. She had seen the Grand Teton in all its moods and had long had a great desire to reach the summit. In many conversations, I encouraged her and empathized with her ambition. I was determined to help her get to the top of the mountain she loved.

Still, I thought over her request for a while because now she was asking me to be a real guide. I knew we would have to be organized about it. On the East Ridge, I had seen what disorganization could lead to; it practically lost me my life. The havoc of the Owen expedition was fresh in my mind. I was not going to have any more of that. So I cautiously told her yes, I would take her up and said I thought she could make it if we took dead aim at things. If we went slowly and the weather was all right, she would have a good chance.

I packed up my things, and she drove me back to her place and put me up in her guest cabin. We started to plan her expedition. I told her we should get Ike Powell with his pack outfit to take us up the trail I had scouted out to get horses into the canyon below the Middle Teton. To get a good jump on the mountain, though, we would have to make camp even further up the canyon than before.

Ike Powell had told me after the last trip that he would sure like to go to the top of the Grand Teton sometime. Geraldine thought it was a good idea to have Ike along and said Jack Crawford, who had been on the first Owen climb, could come along too.

So that was the group. I had some new rope to take along and, of course, I insisted we take extra clothing, although I didn't plan on being caught out at night in a storm again if I could help it. I carefully explained to Geraldine that we had to watch the time and weather closely, and we would be conservative and would retreat if necessary. But if that was the case it was nothing, because there would always be another day.

Once we had gathered our equipment and Ike had brought his horses up to Geraldine's place, we were ready to go. Ike was accompanied by an assistant to watch over the horses at timberline. Early the next morning we headed up what Ike was now calling the "Petzoldt Trail" into Garnet Canyon.

I had started calling it Garnet Canyon after the unusual number of huge garnets protruding from the canyon rocks that Mr. Owen had pointed out to me. It was originally Bradley Canyon, just a name extension of Bradley Lake. Later, I collected some of the garnets I found there and sold one for twenty-five dollars. I would like to have it back today. It was not a perfect garnet, but it was almost as big as my head. I've never seen one that large since.

We had a saddle horse for everyone and three or four pack horses, so it was quite a string going up. I even rode a horse myself. That night we camped at timberline. The next day we left the horses with Ike's assistant and started off on foot, carrying with us only what we needed to spend one more night on the mountain. I planned to camp above the waterfall that dropped down near the big meadow east of the Middle Teton.

On my previous two trips, I'd seen huge rocks lodged above the waterfall. They were as big as houses. Underneath the rocks on the lower side was an overhang. It was possible to crawl back underneath that overhang to a perfectly dry place protected from the wind, rain, and snow. Eventually these became known as the Petzoldt Caves and were a regular stopping point for future guided trips of mine.

I had noticed when climbing that drinking plenty of water and snacking along the way increased endurance — I didn't know why back then. During the climb, I encouraged Geraldine and the others to drink and snack on candy or a sandwich to keep up their energy.

Despite our careful pace, we were able to reach our destination above the big falls quite early in the afternoon. We rolled some rocks out from underneath the overhanging ledge and cleared a large enough space for our blankets. After dinner, just as the sun was setting behind the Lower Saddle, Geraldine and I went out on the edge of the cliff, where we could see the waterfall. The top of the Grand Teton was bathed in the orange light of the evening, which Geraldine called alpenglow. She looked at me and asked, "Do you think I can really make it?"

"I think you can," I said. "You climb well with those new boots with the soft hobnails. They're a little heavy, but you seem to handle them fine."

She seemed satisfied with my answer so I changed the subject. "It's been a wonderful day," I said. "I hope I don't ask too many questions, but there are a lot of things I don't know about this country. What you tell me about the people, the places, and the animals here — I really appreciate it."

Geraldine had told me the names of several flowers we passed during our climb. She was especially enthusiastic about the Indian paintbrush and the little buttercups that grew up as soon as the snow melted. There were so many flowers and there was so much to know. I was inquisitive and my curiosity paid off. Later, when I became a full-time guide, I was the one identifying the plants and animals, which made the climbs more interesting for my clients.

The next morning we were up early. I explained to the group before we started that I was going to set the pace and that we were going to go slowly with frequent stops.

Ike and Crawford carried some of the extra gear. Ike was crippled, with one leg shorter than the other, but still managed to be a real cowboy and to show great balance and endurance as he climbed.

I was in the lead with Geraldine directly behind me so she could follow in my footsteps and imitate my climbing style. It was late summer, but there was still a lot of snow on the Grand Teton. This was a great advantage, because we could cross the snowfields with less energy than it took to climb over rough boulders or to step up and down over big rocks. Everyone had an alpenstock to help maintain balance as we climbed.

There was a friendly smell of spring in the air. The rotting of last year's grass and flowers and the odor of the new flowers and new growth permeated the atmosphere. Spring follows the snowfields up the mountains. At the edge of the snowfields, where the snow is melting, it feels like spring even though it was August hot in the valley. Crows sailed high above and then closed their wings and dove in playful falls, sometimes turning over and spreading their wings again to sail even higher on the western breeze.

We reached the bottom of the glacier that lies on the northeast side of the Middle Teton. There, where the glacier met the rock, was a safe place to walk. The snow was firm though soft from the day's sun, and it was easy to kick steps close together. It was perfect for Geraldine. As we went up the glacier, the snow became steeper and steeper. I put the rope on Geraldine to belay her up. The others followed, and soon we got off the snow onto the flowered lower slopes of the Lower Saddle. There we paused in the mild breeze for a drink from a little rivulet that ran out from underneath the snow. We ate our sandwiches and shared a can of sardines.

Geraldine was fascinated by the work of some nearby coneys. On my first ascent, Ralph had not known why these animals were called coneys, so I asked Geraldine if she knew. "I've always called them coneys because they are mentioned several times in the Bible," she said.

After our snack, we continued to where the black streak crosses the saddle. Many people viewing similar streaks from the valley, like the one straight up the Middle Teton or on Mount Moran, think it is coal. It is a different kind of rock than the hard granite-type rock normally found in the Teton Range. It tends to be brittle and to break into square chunks. I've heard that in ancient geologic times it was intruded underneath the earth's surface before the mountains were raised up to their present height.

We went along the same route Ralph and I had followed, pioneered by the Owen party in 1898. By using a rope and kicking deep steps in the snow we made our way slowly toward the Upper Saddle. About that time Ike, who was bringing up the rear, said there were four people following our trail.

"They seem to be coming very fast, and it looks like they're traveling light," he said. "Do you think everybody in Jackson's Hole is going to try and run up here now?"

"I don't know," I said. "But we're not going to stop and wait for them. Let's keep going."

Slowly, we kept kicking our steps in the snow using the rope for protection when necessary. Finally, we made it to the Upper Saddle. To our right towered the vertical West Face of the Grand Teton. I explained how we could bypass it by following the route the Owen party had discovered twenty-six years earlier.

By this time, the party of four was almost on our heels. I wondered what we would do when they caught up with us. Would we explain the route to them? Would we let them go ahead and risk the possibility of their dislodging some stones that might be dangerous to us below? Or would we try to encourage them to follow behind us and go at the slow pace necessary for us, when they probably wanted to race up to the top?

As they approached, I noticed they were not prepared for an overnight stay, even at timberline. They hadn't ridden this kind of horse before. They had little extra clothing and weren't carrying a rope. Since the locals had not climbed mountains with ropes, they probably thought they could just run up to the top and back, which they could if they wanted to take chances. But I knew some places coming down where a rope would be handy for them and would ensure their safety. Beginners doing the climb without having climbed before and without rope were playing poker with their lives.

When they caught up to us Geraldine recognized them, and there were introductions and handshakes all around. The four men were Allen Budge, Frank Edmiston, Albert Gunther, and Joe May of Kelly, Wyoming. They were carrying a piece of lodgepole pine that looked like a short tepee pole. They said they had a United States flag, and they wanted it waving in the wind from the top of the Grand Teton so their friends from Kelly could see it — to prove they'd been up there. We all thought that was a noble thing to do. I suggested we join forces for the remainder of the climb, and if they had any difficulties carrying the pole, we could assist them with our rope.

Before proceeding, the four men wanted to examine the Enclosure and get a better look at the final part of the ascent. I encouraged them to go up to the Enclosure, because I thought when they saw the frightening view of the last few hundred feet of the climb, they would be bluffed out of continuing. The rest of us moseyed across the Upper Saddle, and by the time we reached the Belly Roll two of them had caught up to us again. I'd been half right. May and Gunther decided they had gone far enough, but Budge and Edmiston were still game and agreed to accompany us to the top.

I put Crawford on the rope first and sent him around the Belly Roll to the platform in front of the Crawl. Next, I put Geraldine on the rope and belayed her from around a rock so I knew I could catch her if she fell. Without hesitation she took hold of the top of the slab and climbed around with grim determination. As she hung on to the top of the rock and started to put her feet down on the other side, I instructed Crawford to plant her feet on the footholds that she could not see. With Crawford's help, she made it.

I belayed Ike over and then came over myself. The four of us stood on the platform, crowded but safe. We did not mention the drop below, but I saw the others looking at the tops of pine trees three thousand feet down with some apprehension. Budge and Edmiston had to wait to come around the Belly Roll until we had crossed the Crawl; there just wasn't enough room on the platform for all of us.

I instructed Crawford to go first over the Crawl. There is really no danger of crossing it; it's just a mental hazard. Geraldine was next. She stayed well on the inside of the ledge, so there wasn't any danger of her falling off. Once we were all across, I took the lead and scrambled up the chimney, over the chockstone, and around the corner where I knew there was a superb belay.

Geraldine tied on to the other end of the rope. Ike and Crawford helped boost her up so she could get ahold of the inside of the chockstone. With them lifting and pushing up on her feet she was able to squirm into the crack. She had little difficulty in pressing on both sides of the crack and wiggling up to where I was. From there, I had her go up a ways to a comfortable place, belaying her from below, then I helped the others.

I carefully belayed Geraldine up over the more difficult places and the others were either belayed or they hung on to the rope to avoid an accident. And any accident there is fatal. Anyone who fell wouldn't have stopped until he or she had reached the pine trees below.

The second and last chimney we had to climb was a bit more difficult, but with tugging from above and some pushing from below, we were able to coax Geraldine through it. From there to the top was a scramble over rocks and snow, but the area was exposed in many places and protection was essential. I kept Geraldine on the rope and she followed directly behind me. When we got a few feet from the top I stopped, took ahold of

Geraldine's hand, and brought her around to the front. I patted her on the back and urged her to the summit first.

She was silent as she looked down at her cabin, a speck way below. As I came up, she grabbed me and hugged me. I thought perhaps I heard soft crying. But as the others arrived, Geraldine regained her composure. I don't think she often broke through her protected personality, but in that moment when she threw her arms around me with a soft sob, I sensed the real Geraldine Lucas, an intelligent, loving woman who had elected for some reason to leave most of society behind.

From the moment Mr. Owen introduced her to me, I felt a closeness with her. I respected and admired her way of life and sensed that underneath her tough exterior was a woman who really cared about people, but perhaps had been hurt by some circumstances in her past. I felt proud of having helped this wonderful person to the top of the Grand Teton, something she had wanted to do for a long, long time.

When the others arrived at the top there was shouting, conversation, and lots of activity. I, for one, felt relief. I sat down on the edge of the summit in silence looking down at Jackson's Hole, letting the others do what they wished. Soon they had fastened the flag on top of the flagpole and had piled up rocks around it so it was secure.

Then the rounds of picture taking started. It was a patriotic moment and I will remember forever one shot of Geraldine standing on top, her arms outspread, with the flag flying behind her. Another picture I will never forget is one in which I stepped out in front of the group and assumed an artificial heroic pose, as if I were claiming the top of the Grand Teton for the queen of England: "I claim thee for your majesty, the queen."

While the others were celebrating and putting their names in containers to leave as a record, I was thinking seriously about the descent. When it was time to depart, I reminded everyone that we needed to be careful not to overturn any rocks that might fall down on another climber in the party. We came down in stages. I supervised the descent, and in many places we fastened the rope so the others could use it as a handhold. When Geraldine went down I belayed her.

Geraldine Lucas on the summit of the Grand Teton with Jack Crawford in the foreground during Paul's second guided ascent and third trip, 1924. Lucas was the second woman to reach the top of the Grand. (Teton County Historical Center)

Traveling slowly, we managed to reach the Upper Saddle without incident. I could sense the others were anxious to leave us, so we bid them good-bye. The four men took off at great speed hoping to get all the way down to the valley that night. They had started early that morning and didn't have the supplies to spend the night.

We kept up our slow and steady place and belayed Geraldine down the steep snow slope below the Lower Saddle to the safety of the lower part of the Middle Teton glacier. It was easy then to follow our own footsteps down to the end of the glacier and to start over the boulders again.

Geraldine was very tired and was becoming quite weak. She needed a little bit more support as we went along, but she never complained. We arrived at the safety and comfort of our camp just as full darkness was setting in. Though quite exhausted, Geraldine was in fine spirits and joined in the conversation and laughter as we ate our dinner with great appetites and retired to our blankets for a sound sleep. I closed my eyes that night with a head full of ideas. I had definitely decided that guiding was in my future.

***

When Billy Owen heard Geraldine had made it to the top, he was determined to do so too. On the eve of my second expedition with Billy Owen, about a week after the first one, we camped at the bottom of Death Canyon between the White Grass and JY dude ranches. We wanted a full day's start going up Death Canyon. While we sat around the campfire that night, Mr. Owen told stories about his boyhood growing up in Wyoming and early years in the Tetons.

One of his more interesting tales was of learning to ride a bicycle as a young man in Laramie, Wyoming. In those days, bicycles had one big wheel in front and a little wheel in back and were powered by pedals attached directly to the front wheel. As he rode his bicycle along the wagon roads of Wyoming he often camped with cowboys tending to the herds of cattle that roamed the open range. Of course, the bicycle was a peculiarity and a source of great amusement and jokes among the cowboys.

However, when Mr. Owen challenged the cowboys, saying he could ride a bucking horse but they couldn't ride his bicycle, they fought over who would get the first try. The cowboys' rides never lasted more than a few feet, so Mr. Owen had the last laugh.

His real adventure on his bicycle came when he rode it through Yellowstone Park in the days of the stagecoaches that took the dudes from the railroad stations in West Yellowstone and Montana through the park. Here he was on his high-wheeled bicycle on the park's barely maintained roads, arousing much curiosity among the dudes and rangers. Mr. Owen on his bicycle was a nemesis to bears, who ran pell-mell into the woods on his approach. "Had no trouble with the grizzlies when I rode that bicycle," he said.

After coming through the park, Mr. Owen headed for Fort Hall in Idaho. It was then that he got his first full view of the Tetons, a little further north but similar to the first view Ralph and I had of the Tetons. He said he looked at them for a long time and decided, as we had, that he was going to climb the Grand Teton one day.

I was thrilled to hear stories about Mr. Owen's youth and the early history of the Tetons. I wondered if I could keep this energetic man at a slow-enough pace up the Grand Teton to keep his heart beating within the range that Dr. Huff had prescribed. There was no doubt about his climbing skill, but the success of the climb would depend not upon our mountaineering ability but on our ability to keep his heartbeat under a certain number.

I found it hard to sleep that night, and my excitement had me up before Ike the next morning. The trail through Death Canyon was rugged, and I preferred to lead my horse so I could look down over the edge of the trail standing on my own two feet rather than from high atop a horse. We passed through the canyon and onto some slopes covered solidly with flowers and grass. That night we camped at the little lake at the head of Teton Creek that flowed down to Driggs, Idaho.

It was a warm day, and there wasn't a cloud in the sky. I was restless, so I told Mr. Owen I was going to scout the trail ahead. As I headed toward the Grand, the South Teton loomed on my right.

The reason I went toward the South Teton was to go up to the top of the grassy slope that led toward Cascade Canyon, to see if it was possible to get the horses down into the upper part of the canyon. I thought it might be possible, because Mr. Owen said that in the earliest days, sheepherders from Pierre's Hole had run sheep into Cascade Canyon, which funnels into Jenny Lake. But he didn't know whether that trail was still passable on horseback.

So that was my reason for running out of camp. I wasn't running out of there to climb the South Teton. When I got to the boulder field leading down into Cascade Canyon, I could see it was probably possible, if we rolled a few rocks out of the way, to get the pack outfit through there. But then right there were the slopes of the South Teton just beckoning me. I took off at a run and galloped over the boulders and up the climbable cliffs to the top.

It was not a first ascent. A cairn had been left by Albert Ellingwood the year before. I got a good look at the Grand and then hurried back, since I had been gone quite a while. Ike and Mr. Owen were surprised that I had climbed all the way to the top of the South Teton, but I was full of energy.

While Ike was cooking dinner and Mr. Owen was napping I committed a sin. I couldn't resist carving my name and the year in a nearby tree. I had done this before on a Douglas fir at the foot of Garnet Canyon on the first Owen expedition. Carving names and initials was quite customary in the early days. After all, I think some of the great treasures of Yellowstone are the pieces cut out of trees with Colter's name on them. Mr. Owen and others had carved their initials in a rock on top of the Grand Teton.

One of the first picture books my sister gave me when I was growing up had a picture of a tree with the name Daniel Boone carved in the side. I was motivated by the romantic notion of leaving my name on one of the great trees of the Tetons. When I visited the spot fifty years later it had grown over beautifully, and the letters had become artistically colored with age. After carving my name, I returned to the fire to have a snack with Ike while Mr. Owen slept.

We were up pretty early the next morning and we didn't figure it was going to be a long day, because the distance wasn't very far, certainly not more than a couple or three miles. The packs had to be put on very solidly, because we knew we were going through some rough country. We rode up the grassy, flowered slopes to the top of the pass into Cascade Canyon. There was a saddle there between some cliffs of sedimentary rock and the slopes leading up the South Teton. The saddle separated the drainages of Teton Creek that ran down to Driggs from what is now called Avalanche Canyon, which holds a stream that flows down into Taggart Lake.

On the other side of the pass we had to descend a few hundred feet through a mass of boulders, where the sheepherders had rolled the boulders around so the horses could get through a series of small switchbacks down to the grassy slopes that led over to the Middle Teton. Stopping there, we had to roll some more rocks off the trail so that the horses didn't get their hooves stuck in the cracks between boulders, which could cause them to bruise or even break a leg.

That took us some time, but after that it was just picking our way through a series of grassy slopes and gentle ledges. We were able to take the horses all the way over right to the base of the Middle Teton on the west, where the cliffs rose practically straight up from a little isolated lake that lay in a little depression. We named the place Alaska Basin because it was full of snow and flowers were blooming and that's the way I imagined Alaska was way up north. There we camped.

There was feed for the horses, and Ike hobbled them and turned them loose but kept one tied up out of habit. He'd let one graze a little bit, but at night he would tie it up so he would always have a horse to ride in the morning in case the others had strayed away. Even with their hobbles on, horses learned to leap with their two front feet together like a kangaroo and some of them could travel miles at night. Homers — those horses that always wanted to go home — didn't make good packhorses. They were generally eliminated from a pack string, if possible, because if they started home every night and spent all night leaping around on the trail, going back instead of getting their guts full of grass, they tended to take the other horses with them.

The next morning the horses were rounded up, hobbled, and one was left tied to a small tree while we were up on the Grand Teton. First, we had to get up over a rocky saddle and do some real climbing, with a rope for safety, to reach the glacier that lies under the west side of the Lower Saddle. Then we crossed that glacier over to a chute that runs down from the black streak. Mr. Owen had to be restrained when we reached the walkable part of the glacier. If I had let him take the lead, he would have made the top in no time, his heart willing. So I set the pace. But even with the reduced rate it wasn't long before we reached the Upper Saddle.

If it were up to me we would have gone straight to the summit, but Mr. Owen wanted to see the Enclosure first. I thought that was something we could do on the way back if he still had the energy, but he did not seem tired. So we scrambled to the top of the highest pinnacle of the Grand Teton and observed the summit from there.

"If you study the mountain from here, it's hard to see where the 'cooning' place is," Mr. Owen said. "You only see the overhang and the drop down into Cascade Canyon. You wouldn't suspicion there was a ledge there."

Before we left the Enclosure, Mr. Owen showed me where he had chiseled his name in one of the rocks on one of his summit attempts before 1898. He was amazed at how clear and legible it still was after all those years.

As we traversed the Upper Saddle toward the Belly Roll, I noticed that Ike was not climbing with as much enthusiasm as he had before lunch. He had had a fight with the game warden the night before we left. I knew it was difficult for him to breath through his swollen nose, and he looked like he was coming down with a little mountain sickness.

So as not to endanger him, the three of us agreed that he should wait for us at the Upper Saddle, and Mr. Owen and I continued on. I belayed Mr. Owen safely around the Belly Roll. The crack in back of the Belly Roll gave the rope a natural belay for me to scramble over to join him. I was at ease, although I was aware that a fall without the rope would mean certain death. I wasn't going to let the danger hinder my ability to climb or to guide Mr. Owen.

When I joined Mr. Owen he said, "There it is, the 'cooning' place. We never thought to look around this corner in the early days."

When he had wiggled across the Crawl, I joined him. We were in great spirits, almost laughing at our success. This part of the climb was becoming second nature to me now. When I made it to the spot in the chimney where I could belay Mr. Owen, he asked me to give him a tug so he could reach the first handhold. He wasn't tall enough to grab it on his own.

Mr. Owen climbed smoothly, flowing over the rocks like an old cat. As I watched him climb I thought, I hope I can do that when I'm his age. All that remained after the second chimney were a series of small pitches with no real belaying necessary, only in the more difficult places.

For the last bit of the climb I lagged behind so Mr. Owen could go first, and when he got to the top he straightened up and said, "I never thought I'd get up here again. This is wonderful."

I quickly joined him, and we sat in silence for a while looking toward Yellowstone and the panorama of Jackson's Hole with its many beautiful lakes.

"In '98," Mr. Owen said, "when we got near the summit we all stopped and we agreed that we should go slowly and look over every rock for anything that was disturbed, anything to indicate that somebody had been there before. We carefully, very carefully walked to the summit. Not one rock was in an unnatural position. Not one rock was on top of another. No debris of any kind. No scratches on the rocks. No container that might have names in it, absolutely nothing unnatural about the peak.

"When we got to the top I think Reverend Spalding was the first to say, 'We are the first people to set foot on top of the Grand Teton.' That is when we decided, all of us, with clear consciences, that we were the first to reach the top of the Grand Teton."

Mr. Owen looked at the old Rocky Mountain Club pennant. "Spalding brought that from Colorado," he said. "When I saw you in the square after your first ascent, and you described it and described all these holes in the top where it had been hit by lightning, I had no doubt that you had been to the top."

While Mr. Owen gazed at the Wind Rivers and reminisced about his surveying days there, I rechiseled his name in the rock where it had worn away since 1898.

We had reached the summit at noon and after an hour on top we slowly descended the mountain by the same route. On a few occasions, I protected Mr. Owen by belaying. He never slipped or showed any sign of starting to fall. When we came to the chimney where he had to hang on to the chockstone and slide backward over the edge, his feet would not quite reach the ground. I gave him a snug rope until he landed on solid rock. We went back across the Crawl and around the Belly Roll and met up with Ike.

Carefully and steadily, the three of us made our way down the mountain. Soon we were over the last ridge. There below us, a short distance away, was our friendly camp in the scrub pines on the west shores of Sunset Lake that hugged the Middle Teton. We practically jumped over the boulders and ran down to camp. Mr. Owen no longer needed to count his heartbeats.

The day had been a glorious one and one that I knew I would always remember. What a great privilege it was to have climbed with such a man as Mr. Owen. He had been my friend and champion. After listening to Ralph's and my story he had enthusiastically encouraged us to go up the Grand Teton, which started me out on a new career and established me as a person in society. I was noticed and talked about and already had a good reputation, which I enjoyed. I was accepted as part of the community in Jackson's Hole. I'd found a home.

Everyone who met Mr. Owen seemed to love him. Everyone called him Billy Owen, and you could tell by the way they greeted him how much they admired him. He was a hero in Wyoming. I didn't know anybody who seemed to have a better reputation or was loved by everyone. As long as I was in Wyoming, I never heard a native of Wyoming say anything derogatory about Billy Owen. My being of help to such a wonderful and famous man filled me with elation. To me, it was like a young baseball player of my day going out camping with Babe Ruth, or some starstruck gal going out camping with Mary Pickford. 'Cause here I was with my hero, and everybody's hero.

We had no sooner sat down than Ike had a fire blazing, and he took a blue enamel coffee pot and poured Mr. Owen and me two tin cups almost full of boiling coffee. Then he went over to his pack and brought back a bottle. I think I read Jack Daniel's on the label. He finished filling the coffee cups with the liquid poured out of the bottle, and a new aroma swept over the landscape.

"You fellas deserve this," he said. "Mighty fine job you did today, and I think it's time for us to relax and celebrate a little. You may not know it, Mr. Owen, but I knew all along that today was your birthday. You are sixty-five years old today and what a celebration it must be for you to climb the Grand Teton again."

I was astonished to hear that it was Mr. Owen's birthday, but when Ike started to sing "Happy Birthday" I joined in. We sang robustly and loud, and the second after we finished singing we heard "you" bounce back from the nearby cliffs of the Middle Teton. Ike mixed himself a tin cup full of the new Middle Teton elixir and went back to cooking supper. We satisfied our honest hunger with large numbers of hot biscuits smeared with butter, fried smoke-cured ham, and big Idaho russet potatoes that were baked in the hot coals at the edge of the fire.

CHAPTER THREE

HOW TEPEE'S GLACIER GOT ITS NAME

"Climbing is easy until it becomes impossible."
— *Paul Petzoldt*

My second summer of climbing didn't start out well. I returned to Jackson's Hole with Ralph, who I knew had been as anxious as I to do some more climbing. I also invited a good Mormon friend of mine from Twin Falls, Melvin Whitehead, to come along with us. He was one of my climbing companions in the Snake River Canyon.

In late July, as soon as we arrived in Jackson's Hole, we went straight to the Jenny Lake campground. Melvin was anticipating a trip up the Grand Teton. I thought we might get some guiding that summer, but no clients were available at the time. We decided to scout the East Ridge. Our plan was to get around the corner of the first pinnacle, now called the Molar Tooth, either by revisiting where Ralph and I had spent the horrible night on our first climb or by looking again at the possibility of the north traverse.

It was going to be a great, fun trip. I had observed the mountain a good deal on my other trips and was convinced that if we got around the Molar Tooth, the East Ridge would be quite climbable the rest of the way. It would be a more direct way to the top of the Grand Teton than the Owen Route.

We made thorough preparations. Along with our good shoes, we had better clothing than we had worn before, including extra jackets. We took gloves, good rope, and an adequate amount of food. While we were making our plans, we met a young man in the campground who was interested in joining us. He introduced himself as Harold Criger. He had some time before he was going to a job in Alaska and had done some climbing, so we invited him along.

He had some of his own equipment and, like us, had boots with soft hobnails driven into their leather soles, which were practical for climbing in the Tetons because the hard Teton rock bit into the soft iron of the hobnails, which made for a secure purchase.

We hiked up to Delta Lake, where we revisited our beautiful camp from the year before. Criger, who was thinking about his trip to Alaska, kept asking us about bears, and we told him we had never had any bear problems in the Tetons. We had discovered a bear den on our first trip on a ridge below Delta Lake, but in all my trips up the mountain I had not seen a bear track. That may have been because sheepherders didn't allow bears to exist if they could help it. They had rifles with them at all times and to them, a good bear was a dead bear.

The next day, all of us being in good shape, we were up to the Molar Tooth in a short time. We took a look at the north traverse first. Even though I was used to heights by this time, it was frightening looking down that section of the North Face onto the glacier way below. We didn't expect the mountain to be crowded, so we rolled off a couple rocks. It seemed to take forever for them to reach the bottom.

Ralph wanted to lead so I let him. I tied on to the other end of his rope and belayed him from below. As the leader, Ralph didn't have a belay from above. I wasn't watching him very closely and he, like many climbers without much experience leading, reached a spot about twenty-five feet above me where he got stuck and couldn't move up or down.

He was hanging on by his fingers and had some meager footholds. Then his legs started to shake. His knees wobbled as I had seen happen with some of my boyhood friends climbing in the Snake River Canyon. I felt that he was going to come off any time. I wrapped my end of the rope around a rock nearby to be sure that the only way he was going to slide down off the North Face was if the rope broke. To help break his fall, I belayed the rope in front of the rock.

Harold Criger, Paul, and Melvin Whitehead on Paul's first attempt at the summit in 1925, which was cut short by Ralph Herron's fall. Photo taken by Ralph Herron. (American Heritage Center, University of Wyoming)

He started to slide down and bump over the rocks; it wasn't a direct fall. I took in the rope as he came down. He landed near my feet and then bounced over the edge. I couldn't catch him there, but I had brought in the rope enough to shorten the rest of his fall. He dropped about another ten feet before I caught him with the belay.

Ralph was severely injured and in great pain. We went down to him to see what we could do. I thought at the time he might be very seriously hurt, because he complained of pain in his chest and shoulder and also in one leg near the knee. We managed to bring him back up to where we could all stand and we made him as comfortable as possible.

He passed out a few times because of the pain, but in a couple of minutes he had recovered enough to move his arms and shoulders, so we knew there weren't any breaks. His chest still hurt, which indicated he might have a cracked rib, but the main problem was his knee. When we finally raised him up to his feet he couldn't put any weight on that foot.

We wrapped the knee to keep it from moving too much, but it wasn't really splinted. We did have it slightly bent because at that time there was only one way we had of carrying him — piggyback. We didn't have any artificial stretcher or anything like that in those days, and we wouldn't have had one along anyway.

While descending the East Ridge, we avoided the big boulders by going around to the north. With some help from Criger and Whitehead, who protected Ralph and me with the rope on the steep places, I was able to carry him down to our camp at Delta Lake. It was a terrible night for Ralph. We had no painkillers to give him. He had fitful periods of sleep, but he was in continuous pain.

At daylight the next morning, we stabilized the knee again as much as we could. We traveled as fast as the terrain and our strength would allow, down to Geraldine's ranch. Ralph showed terrific character by enduring the pain without complaint. A medic from the Double Diamond Ranch nearby came up and treated Ralph as best he could before he was brought to the hospital in Jackson and placed under the care of Dr. Huff. He had suffered some cracked ribs and a severely sprained and bruised knee. After a few days in the hospital he was out walking on crutches, and by the end of the summer was walking naturally again.

I headed back to the Jenny Lake campground and then from there to the hayfields. Criger left for upper Jackson's Hole, where he was staying. Later that summer I guided Criger to the top of the Grand Teton. Whitehead had work to do in Twin Falls with his family and had a summer job, so he took off for home.

***

I had become well acquainted with Gibb Scott when we climbed the Grand Teton together with Billy Owen during my first summer in the Tetons. At that time, he proved to be a natural leader who used sound judgment. Since he was a packer and a guide and popular with the dudes, especially the lady dudes, I thought then that he might start climbing the Grand Teton as a business. I wondered if I was going to have some competition.

One night, about a week after Ralph's accident, I was in bed asleep at the Lucas ranch when I was suddenly awakened about midnight by Bill Lucas with a lantern in his hand. I practically jumped out of bed wondering what the hell was wrong. He told me the sheriff had just called and I was to get up and get my mountain gear ready because there had been somebody killed up on the glacier in the Tetons. I was supposed to go up with the deputy sheriff to help bring down the body.

I wondered who was killed up there, whether it was a local person learning how to climb or if it was some dude. Bill Lucas told me Gibb Scott had taken a party up to the top of the Grand Teton and one of them was killed on the way down. That was all the sheriff had told him. As I threw on my mountain-climbing clothes and boots and started to pack up my gear, I wondered where the fella was and how we were going to get him down and who was going to help me.

I was a little bit flattered that they had called on me, but I wasn't necessarily enthused about going up there with some local cowboys to bring somebody off some cliff on the Grand Teton. One thing that I was sure of, and I was going to tell the deputy sheriff when he first arrived, was that if I went up there to help bring down a body, I was going to be in charge. When I told him this he agreed. "I don't know anything about climbing and you do," he said. "You're the only one available right now that knows anything about it, so you've got to lead this party up there and bring this guy down. I'll help you, but you can sure call the shots as far as I'm concerned."

That was Joe Nethercott, the deputy sheriff, and as soon as he arrived I jumped in his car and we sped off down the road. In the meantime, Mrs. Lucas had gotten up and cooked me some pancakes and had given me a couple cups of coffee. She told me I would need my strength, and it was the truth.

Off we went toward Jenny Lake. They used to say, "Don't spare the horses." Well, we didn't spare the car. We jumped over the ruts in the wagon road as it wound through the sagebrush up toward Menor's Ferry. Sometimes on particularly big bumps all four wheels of the car left the ground, landing with dust flying in all directions, scaring the nighthawks off the ground near the road where they had been roosting after catching their bellies' fill of bugs and insects that evening.

We drove mostly in silence, although all sorts of questions were running through my head. Finally, we arrived at Menor's Ferry, and as the deputy flicked the lights of the car on and off, through cupped hands I gave my best mountain yoo-hoos and yodels that I'm sure they heard as far as Jenny Lake. Soon a light appeared in the house across the river, and somebody emerged with a lantern and rode the ferry to our side. When we got on the ferry Bill Menor wanted to know what the hell we were doing at this time of night crossing the river. We told him a man had been killed up on the Tetons and that we were going to bring down the body.

Bill Menor said he'd been expecting something like this for a long time, and maybe I had too. "Well, it will probably happen again. The more people who are interested in climbing that mountain, the more people who are going to be killed. I know that," he said.

"Mountains aren't as dangerous as horses," I said. "A horse can throw you off and you can hit your head on a rock and that's harder than a snowfield. Besides that, they can get you against a rock and some of them will just deliberately squeeze you. I had a horse one time that I took hunting, and he would watch me and every time we went under a tree and I leaned forward he would rear his head back and hit mine and try to knock me off. Besides that, they can bite your arm off. And I know several old cowboys that have been kicked in the wrong place and it's hurt a long, long time."

In spite of the seriousness of the situation, we had a good laugh about the vicious horses we'd known in our lives.

Bill Scott, Gibb's older brother, was shaken and silent when we met him near Geraldine's cabin. He had Jimmy Mangus with him, a local guide and hunter. In hushed tones, as if he were in a funeral parlor, Bill described the situation to me. The man had slipped on the big snowfield below what Billy Owen called the Otter's Body, had slid down and lost control. He started rolling over the steep snow and hit a sharp rock protruding from the snow. The rock had crushed his skull, and he was killed instantly. After getting the news down and notifying the sheriff, Gibb had gone back up the mountain to his pack string at Amphitheater Lake. From there he was going back up to the snowfield, where the dead man's companion, W. D. Young, had stayed all night with the body.

Gibb took with him a couple of mantas and some extra pack ropes so the body could be tied up in the mantas, slid down the snow, and then carried off the mountain. Mantas were heavy pieces of canvas used to cover the loads on a packhorse. The deputy informed Bill and Jimmy that I was going to lead the way up there and that I was in charge of the operation. With that Bill said, "That's sure all right with me. The quicker we get him down and get off that mountain the better I'll feel. I wasn't cut out for work like this. I'm sure glad we have you along. You've been up there a few times and you've got a reputation as being a pretty sensible kid."

We strapped our gear onto some Trapper Nelson packs of Bill's and took off toward the glacier and the ordeal that awaited us. By the time we got across the sagebrush flats to the trail up into Garnet Canyon, the sun was rising in the east, casting its full glare on the mountains, bathing the peaks in the orange alpenglow of sunrise.

We walked in silence and I took the lead. I felt the feet in back of me almost touching my heels, an indication that the others wanted to hurry. The first time we stopped I gave a little lecture. "Fellas, we've got a big day ahead of us," I said. "If we just go slowly now and breathe deeply and conserve our energy and take short steps, we'll be fresh enough when we get there to bring down the body. We don't know yet how much energy that's going to take. It may take a helluva lot."

After that they were content to travel at my pace. We followed the new trail where I had led Ike Powell's pack outfit up into the canyon on the first Owen expedition and Geraldine's climb. When we got to the boulders I saw that my companions, probably all hunting guides at one time or another, could jump from rock to rock with great balance.

After passing the Petzoldt Caves, it was a fairly easy hike across the moraine to the snowfield, where we found Gibb and Young. They had not tried to wrap the body in the mantas, and it looked as if Gibb had stopped with his horses at timberline to grab a few winks of sleep. He had been climbing up and down the mountain for almost twenty-four hours and had only arrived at the body a short time before we had.

Silently, I looked up and saw where Theodore Tepee had first started to slide down from the bergschrund, where the sun's reflection had melted out a gap between the glacier and the rock. Further down the glacier there were indentations in the snow where he had lost control and had rolled head over heels down the steep part. I walked a little ways up from where the body lay to a pointed rock still stained with blood and hair, and maybe even a piece of skull.

I supervised wrapping up the body in the mantas with the rope extended on both sides. This way two people could be in the front and two in back to carry the body in places where it could not be slid over the snow or vegetation. Before we started down, I ran over to look at the big snow chute that Ralph and I had come up from Delta Lake on our first climb. I made the decision that, instead of taking the body all the way down through the boulders in Garnet Canyon and then carrying it up the slope to the horses at Amphitheater Lake, it would be much easier to slide the body down the steep but solid snow chute, which went practically all the way down to where we could cut over directly to Amphitheater.

I explained to Gibb that all we would need was for people to steer the body once in a while and we could protect them with rope when necessary. With a rope tied around Tepee's ankles, we lowered the body down the snow chute as far as the rope would reach. With another rope I belayed Gibb down as far as the body was. The others climbed down, not tied to but holding the rope strung between me and Gibb. After everyone was down to the body I climbed down and joined them. We proceeded this way until we reached the bottom of the chute in much less time than I expected. The body was then carried to Amphitheater Lake, where the horses were waiting.

I relaxed; my job was over. When we got the body down to the horses, that was the end of my responsibility. From then on, I let Gibb handle things. I watched silently as they put the body over a pack saddle and roped it on. We started down the mountain on the trail that Gibb had made, some of us riding the extra horses, some of us walking along behind. When we reached the road head, the body was put into the back of the deputy sheriff's car for transportation to the coroner in Jackson. Young accompanied his dead friend to the hospital.

I stayed on because I wanted to talk to Gibb. I knew that he had been taking people up to Surprise and Amphitheater lakes with his horses to view the glaciers or for short hikes, but this was the first time he had taken anyone to the big peak. I could see that this accident had shocked him. He told me what had happened. He said he had kicked and shoveled some steps down the steep part of the slope to where it leveled off and had suggested to Tepee and Young that they follow his lead. But they had made their own decision to go around on the edge of the bergschrund.

Using their ice axes, they started along the ridge of the bergschrund, a sharp edge that dropped off steeply. That was where Tepee slipped and, unable to stop himself with his ice ax, had started to roll. He rolled down and smashed his head on the rock that I had seen sticking out of the snow. It was the only rock in that part of the snowfield, and if he hadn't hit it, he would have eventually stopped where the slope leveled off.

I think Gibb blamed himself for the accident. He told me he should have insisted that they come down the way he had planned. He was sure they would have made it. However, since they were experienced mountaineers who had climbed a lot in Canada and supposedly knew how to stop themselves with their ice axes, he didn't think he had a right to tell them how to climb. He said he wished he'd insisted on it and if he had, perhaps Tepee would still be alive.

I told Gibb, "I guess we'll have to call that snowfield Tepee's Glacier."

"That's a helluva lot better than calling it Gibb Scott's Glacier," he said.

The night after we brought the body down, I returned to the Lucas ranch, bearing with me a new and heightened stature in Jackson's Hole. I was not only the kid who climbed mountains, but I was also the young man to be called on to rescue people from the high peaks.

Ralph's fall had already started the wheels turning in my head about leading climbs and becoming a responsible guide. I had returned to the Tetons that year with more knowledge and better judgment about mountaineering, but didn't yet have the fortitude or brashness to insist upon planning and leading a trip. Ralph's near-fatal accident changed all that. So by the time I was summoned in the middle of the night to bring the first dead man off what I eventually named Tepee's Glacier, I was in the mood to take charge and to make sure no one else was hurt while bringing the body down.

I thought at that time, damn, we're going to have a lot of accidents if people are going to try and climb these mountains without any training. Even when I had used the most awful judgment of my life trying to climb the East Ridge with Ralph, at least I knew how to climb. I could look at a cliff and know whether I could climb it or not and how difficult it was going to be. I was also a gymnast. I could walk a tightrope, turn front flips and back flips, and do the giant swing on the bar.

So I was qualified as a climber. But here were local people who had none of that experience. I was worried that they would attempt to climb the Grand Teton without rope or the proper clothing and shoes. The Grand Teton is not a mountain a person can fool with like that.

In those days, I had started to play a little golf. I thought of an analogy between mountain climbing and playing golf. If a golfer sliced a drive into the lake, it cost him a ball and a couple of strokes. But if a climber sliced on a mountain, that's the last chance he got.

The news of the first death on the Grand Teton was highly publicized throughout the region. The deputy sheriff was quoted in the newspapers as saying that Gibb and I had risked our lives many times in the heroic act of bringing the body off the Tetons. That wasn't quite true, but people sure got that idea. People also got the idea that maybe it wasn't safe up on the mountains. Both locals and dudes were having second thoughts about climbing the Grand Teton, and nobody was even considering trying it without a guide, which was fine with me. Dudes were used to hiring guides to take them on hunting, fishing, and pack trips anyway, so it wasn't a big change for them. For the locals, it was an insult for them to think they needed a guide to take them anywhere, so they had more to get used to.

Later that summer Gibb told me he was going to stick with his horses and packing, and he was not going to try and climb mountains again, ever. I tried to persuade him otherwise. I explained to him that it had been Tepee's choice. He had experience and if he had gone against Gibb's wishes, it was no fault of Gibb's. But it was no use.

This accident cleared the way for me to become the guide of the Tetons. Had Gibb kept on, with his great ability and reputation and his infectious personality, it would have been hard for me to compete with him. At one time I had thought that maybe we could go in together, me with my climbing and him with his pack outfit — that we could start some sort of a business.

But he was very firm. He took the death of Tepee very, very seriously and felt that he had made a mistake in not taking charge of the party. Later on, people begged Gibb to take them to the top of the Tetons, and he wouldn't do it.

It was a big moment in my life.

Gibb was giving himself hell for not taking charge of these people and for not saving their lives. In talking with him, I decided that with any guiding I ever did, I was not going to let any dude, even though he had climbed in Switzerland and other parts of the world, take charge of any of my climbs. I was going to be the leader.

My judgment was being built from horrible mistakes that I had made and that I saw everybody else was apt to make, unless they had some sort of teaching about judgment and about decision making and about careful planning. Since then, that's been the basis of my whole life.

CHAPTER FOUR

THE LAST OF
THE OLD WEST

"The elk have lived and roamed here for years and years free of charge, but now they're finding large portions of the ancestral winter range occupied by ranchers and homesteaders. They are forced to raid haystacks or die, and as it is turning out they are doing a tremendous amount of both."

— *Bertha Chambers Gillette,* Homesteading
with the Elk

Before our first climb, Ralph and I went down to the Crabtree Hotel with our expedition equipment. After a big delicious breakfast, we loaded into the car and shoved off. Every foot traveled was a revelation to us. We really had not seen the Tetons in full view. We were excited about getting around the buttes that hid the Tetons from Jackson and heading north to the upper part of Jackson's Hole, where the Tetons would be fully visible to us for the first time.

As we went along the dusty roads our driver, Newell Haines, treated us as newcomers or dudes visiting the country. He explained it to us as he would to some new arrivals from Philadelphia whom he was taking up to the Bar BC dude ranch.

"That's Flat Crick over there," he said. "Sure is named right. It hardly runs through that field there to the west, and a lot of ducks and geese nest there during the summer. It's kind of a swamp over on the side, and the grass grows belly high. That's why it's so good for the elk in the wintertime. They can scratch around and expose the grass that's been pushed down in the snow. They eat it right to the ground. Damn near lost the elk herd one time when we had those damn tusk hunters in here."

"What's a tusk hunter?" Ralph asked.

"Well, you know elk. They have two ivory tusks and the older they get the more yellow the tusks get and they get these pretty lines around them. The oldest elk or sometimes the elk with the biggest horns have the most beautiful ivory tusks. These guys were in here shooting these elk just for their tusks and leaving them dead out there. They said you could walk a mile out of Jackson on dead elk without ever touching the ground.

"What did they want the tusks for?" Ralph asked.

"Huh, I thought everybody knew that. There's a big Elk Club out there all over the United States, thousands and thousands of them. Every member of that Elk fraternity would like to have a watch fob with some sort of emblem on it and decorated by one or two of those ivory elk tusks. And they pay big money for them. That's why these guys came from all over just to shoot elk for their tusks: to make some money.

"Well, the local people got kind of tired of that and some of them banded together and told the tooth collectors, 'Boys you'd better not let the sun set on your head another day here in Jackson or you're liable to be laying out there with them elk.' By God, the next day they were all gone. That saved the elk herd," Mr. Haines said.

He also told us that too many elk could lead to problems. They needed a place to eat in the wintertime and the farmers didn't want them eating their haystacks. As we drove on we saw haystacks with boards up around them to keep the elk out. When the farmers fed those stacks in the wintertime they took the top off first and then later they had to take the panels down to get the last bit of hay. The elk really hurt the farmers if they didn't protect their haystacks. The area around Flat Creek was a good place to feed the elk. Farmers could cut some hay right there, stack it up, and keep the elk away from their fields.

"Where are the elk now?" I asked.

"They're way back in the hills," Haines said. "They leave here as soon as the first bit of green grass comes through the ground and they slowly follow this green grass up-country. Part of the herd goes to Yellowstone, another part goes up Flat Crick, and the rest of them head for the Gros Ventre and way over there toward the Wind Rivers. They follow that grass way back to timberline. I've seen 'em in the summer up there in the high altitude eating that luscious new grass and then going out on the big snowfields and lying down on the snow. It keeps them cool and there aren't so many flies and bugs out there on the snowfields. Them elk are pretty smart creatures."

Haines then continued with his guided tour. "The road to the north over there with all those farms is called Mormon Row," he said. "Most of the early settlers in here were Mormons. They chose that sagebrush flat because they could plow up the ground and irrigate using water from the mountain streams. Mighty fine people live out there."

***

I didn't know then that I would later hear Will Deloney testify at a Congressional hearing in Jackson with tears in his eyes when he told about the farms we were looking at being burnt to the ground, log houses and barns being torn down, and fields being turned back to sagebrush. This happened when the National Park Service tried to extend its borders to take in much of the choice land of Jackson's Hole.

I was working at the Bill Lucas ranch at the time, must have been the late twenties, and I was acquainted with the people who were going to be put out of business. One of my best friends in Jackson's Hole then was Dick Winger, a relative of Ralph Herron's from Newton, Iowa. He explained to me about the difficulties some of the ranchers were having in what we called up-country, especially up around the Buffalo River toward Togwotee Pass. There, they were very isolated in the wintertime. It probably took two days over the mail-sled route for them to come to Jackson with horses and sleighs. One exceptionally hard winter they were short of hay and there was no way of getting cattle out or getting hay in, so they lost some of the herd. Their calf crops were diminished for a few years and they fell behind in payments to the local bank.

Robert Miller, who was part of the Jackson State Bank at the time, thought it might be practical to get eastern finances interested in Jackson's Hole. He thought maybe people could buy parts of some of those farms for summer homes or private hunting camps or even for increasing the dude business. This was the type of income that Jackson's Hole was already getting. What the banker wanted to do was to expand the business that was already practical in Jackson's Hole: having dudes come there to play cowboy for the summer or to hunt or to have the prestige of owning a little piece of land in the valley. But the real purpose was to get the loans cashed out in the bank, because the bank didn't want to keep carrying questionable loans for these ranchers who were behind in their payments.

So Miller hired Dick Winger to go back East and talk to people about his idea. Dick's main entry was the Campfire Club, which was made up of a group of wealthy easterners. He went there and met with them, as individuals and as a group, trying to sell them the idea of investing in Jackson's Hole and increasing the tax base and perhaps saving the equity the ranchers had in their land.

Nothing much came out of Dick's trip East. But as he told me later, he thought it may have had some influence on Rockefeller, who had done a lot to develop the parks in Maine and other places in the East. The superintendent of Yellowstone Park was friendly with Rockefeller; evidently the Rockefeller group thought supporting the extension of Yellowstone Park to take in the Tetons was a good way of investing their surplus money, by giving it to the park service and not having to pay taxes on it. But as Dick said, and as everybody in Jackson's Hole thought, their real purpose was to improve the reputation of the Rockefeller name, because there was a lot of public feeling against John D. Rockefeller, deserved or not.

In 1924, Mrs. Amoretti, who owned the lodge up by Jackson Lake, came and tried to climb the Grand Teton with the Owen party. That same summer Rockefeller had been down to her ranch as a guest of hers — a paying guest, of course — for the purpose of taking a look at the country and probably making decisions about the feasibility of investing money to expand Yellowstone Park. Dick told me that soon after that, there had been secret meetings between some people from Yellowstone and some people in Jackson's Hole, who wanted the extension of the park to take in Jackson's Hole, or most of it. The people thought the idea then was to bring the boundaries of Yellowstone Park, the west boundary and the east boundary, pretty much straight down: to take in some of the Gros Ventre Mountains, some of the Thorofare country up at the head of the Buffalo River and the west side of the Tetons, and all of the Teton Range, perhaps down as far as Teton Pass or down as far as the town boundaries of Wilson and Jackson.

To many people this was a very noble undertaking. There was a general knowledge in Jackson's Hole that this was being talked about, and this was certainly, some thought, a great ambition for the superintendent of Yellowstone Park. But it didn't take much thought to see that if even the upper part of Jackson's Hole was taken into a park, it would kill the ranching industry there, because the ranchers had to move upward through the valley in order to get to their summer forest leases in the national forest, where they grazed their cattle.

In the summer, they used their irrigated lands in the valley to grow hay, enough hay to feed their cattle through the winter and to calve them out. After the grass started to grow in the spring, they grazed their cows and calves up into the mountains as the snow retreated. It was not possible for ranchers to make a living in Jackson's Hole by having land in the valley for grazing their cows in the summer and having other land in the valley to raise their hay. So extending Yellowstone Park meant the destruction of the agriculture in Jackson. Everyone realized that. That's why many of the people of Jackson's Hole were against park extension. Beside that, the private lands and the private operations — the dude ranches, the guiding services, and what little tourist facilities they had in those days — would all be put out of business. And they were all tax-paying entities that supported the roads and the schools and the towns of Jackson and Wilson.

Around the same time all this was happening, farmers in Idaho had built a big dam on Jackson Lake and raised the lake up to make Jackson Lake much larger than it was before. The building of this dam, the servicing of this dam, and the handling of the water to run it down the Snake River toward the potato fields of Idaho was also an industry that was bringing some money into Jackson's Hole, which was important to its economic stability. If the park got ahold of all the land, people didn't know what would happen to that dam.

So the extension of the park caused not only a fear based on reality, but it also caused a terrific fear of the unknown. If this land was taken over, what would happen to the businessmen of Jackson? What would happen to the bank? What would happen to all the people who lived there, and where would they go? This was a very emotional issue that went to the pocketbooks of most people in Jackson. They were almost ready to get out their guns and fight it out.

The people who settled in Jackson's Hole in the early days were adventurous types — the type who kept moving West with the covered wagon, meeting the unknown, starting lives in new places. Jackson's Hole was sort of the last of the new places. There weren't any more left in the West.

Of course, the congressmen from Wyoming were completely in sympathy with the people of Jackson's Hole, not only because they wanted their votes but because they wanted to protect Wyoming from Yellowstone Park. Yellowstone Park was very unpopular in Jackson and in all of Wyoming, because here was a part of the state that had been taken away and given to the federal government to be run from Washington, D.C. Wyoming citizens couldn't hunt there, they couldn't trap there, and the entrances to Yellowstone Park were either through Idaho to West Yellowstone, which was in Montana, or from the railroads in Montana with spurs and roads that came south. Practically nobody went into the park from Jackson's Hole. There wasn't a good road and there wasn't money to build good roads.

In order to guard against the extension of Yellowstone, the people of Wyoming condescended to have the Tetons made into a park in 1929. They thought if they put that small area of just the Tetons into a national park, then there wouldn't be the national sympathy for Yellowstone to expand to take in the Tetons. Many people believed the Tetons deserved to be in a national park, which they probably did. People also saw it as a way for the forest service to keep most of its land around there, which would be great. That way the little park would not interfere with agriculture or the cattle raising.

While all this was happening, a land company from Salt Lake, called the Snake River Land Company, made its appearance in Jackson's Hole and began buying bits of land. The natives were led to think that this land was going to be for the development of tourism — dude ranches, hunting camps, perhaps private summer homes, and all that kind of stuff that was going to increase the tax revenue of Jackson's Hole. Certain people sold out early, and that brought money into Jackson's Hole. Homer Richards sold his place at Jenny Lake, moved into town, and started building cabin camps for Jackson. So it was helping Jackson's Hole. There was money coming in and it was helping the town, helping the merchants, helping the bank; it seemed to be a good thing.

Winger was hired as one of the agents to buy this land. He told me that he didn't know until later, after he'd bought so much land, that he was buying it for Rockefeller — that Rockefeller was the Snake River Land Company. It was a well-kept secret.

The exposure of the Snake River Land Company ran over Jackson's Hole like an avalanche. The Snake River Land Company was a phoney. It was set up, secretly, to mislead the people of Jackson's Hole, to make them think these were commercial people coming in who would improve the business and the living of the people already in Jackson's Hole. Most important, they thought it would protect the migration routes of the ranch cattle to their summer grazing land.

The reality was entirely different. It was Rockefeller money and it was spent with the intention of destroying all the ranches the company bought, with the intention of eventually eliminating the dude ranches and of eliminating all the local businesses in Jackson's Hole. The company planned to bring down the big corporations that had the concessions in Yellowstone to take over Jackson's Hole with their transportation system, their hotels, their restaurants, and their camera shops. All the junk in Yellowstone was going to be moved right down into Jackson's Hole, and it was going to be one big happy Yellowstone Park.

The banker was fooled. And the people were mad at him for being fooled: He was the one who should have known. And maybe Dick Winger was telling the truth when he said he was fooled too. It was so cleverly masqueraded, and the people of Jackson's Hole felt they were the victims.

I had no inkling about the deal either. I thought it was the Snake River Land Company. They were paying taxes on the land they bought. The burning down of the ranch buildings — there was no indication of that until the news broke.

After it broke, you couldn't go anywhere without hearing people talking about it. There was a terrible feeling and all sorts of bad things were said: "Well, the only reason Rockefeller's doing that is he'd have to give it to the government for taxes." "He's only doing that to make people think that his old man wasn't a thief." I mean, they said awfully bad things about Rockefeller. He was in the same category as mule skinners or people who talked to their horses that were pulling the sleds over Teton Pass.

The whole state of Wyoming was incensed by this trick, and the congressmen were appalled by the way they had been fooled too. Since Congress works by some sort of unwritten but workable connections that senators from different states have with each other, there wasn't any way that Rockefeller was going to give this land to the National Park Service, because other state senators wanted Wyoming's help on certain things.

So here Rockefeller sat with his land, still owned by the Snake River Land Company, I suppose, but Rockefeller had the authority to give this land to the park any day that they would accept it. The people of Wyoming said, "Let him burn down the buildings, but he's not going to get the land put into the park system and he can just keep paying taxes on it from now to eternity."

Then they woke up one morning and found out that money generally wins.

President Roosevelt needed congressional approval to add Rockefeller's land to Teton National Park, but he didn't need congressional approval to turn it into a national monument, which is what he did without warning the senators or any of the public. People in Jackson's Hole thought that it was a secret deal and that they were the suckers.

The day that they were had, residents of Jackson's Hole were so frustrated that a bunch of them got on their horses, got out their guns and revolvers, and went up to the headquarters of Teton National Park. They raced their horses around like Indians around the wagon train, shooting off their rifles, guns, and pistols. There was a picture and a write-up of them in *Time* magazine. But it was hopeless, just hopeless. They were like the Indians circling the wagon train after the buffalo were gone. They had no basis anymore. Their buffalo had been taken away from them.

Even Wallace Beery, who pictured himself as sort of a native of Jackson's Hole because he'd made so many movies there and owned a place up on Jackson Lake, was involved. He was a great friend of the local people and went to the bars and talked freely with them. I was sitting with him one night in the bar having a drink and some woman came up wanting his signature and wanting a picture with him. He did everything she asked, and then she said, "Well, gosh, I bet that you are fed up with all the people like me that bother you all the time."

Wallace said, "If they didn't bother me, I would think I was losing my popularity. I make a living by you bothering me."

So today we have the park, and we have the other part of the valley taken over by the superwealthy, where the common working man can't even live where he works. No wonder a present-day ranger I talked to thought it would have been great if Rockefeller had bought up everything, maybe including Jackson, and put it all in a national park. And at this point, as a Monday-morning quarterback, I agree.

***

The effect on the cattle industry if the park had come down into Jackson's Hole would have been disastrous. The more time I spent in Jackson's Hole, the more I learned about the history and character of the area, including many families' dependence on cattle. Although precarious, cattle provided a simple living that answered the needs of many local people. It was necessary for many ranchers to go through the upper part of Jackson's Hole in the summer, grazing their cattle slowly up along the Snake River to their summer grazing grounds north of Jackson's Hole, almost to the southern edge of Yellowstone.

They'd have a rider out there in the hills who looked after those cattle in the summer and sometimes drove them away from springs and water holes so they wouldn't hurt the ground too much around them and overgraze it. In the fall when it started getting frosty or started to get cold up high, the cattle came down instinctively on their own. The cattle knew the route and the young calves learned it from their mothers. Finally, the cowboys went back and rode the country to get them all out.

Of course, if there were ranchers sharing a certain locality, there might be two or three brands there, and some of those cows might come over and get mixed up. But they didn't leave any up there; if they were with the herd, they'd bring 'em down. They trailed them gently through Jackson's Hole, mostly up close to the park, north of Moran and up toward DuBois, up there on Togwotee Pass. They'd come along the Snake River through those sagebrush places and they'd gradually let them drift down, because they'd be grazing as they came and that saved the ranchers' pastures and hay.

When they got the cattle to the ranch they had a big corral where they'd cut 'em out. That is, Lucas would come, and they'd let all his brand out and he'd have his cowboys drive them away separately toward the Lucas ranch, and then they would cut somebody else's cattle out.

Once in a while they might have one or two that they took all the way to the ranch and maybe they belonged to some people over in DuBois. They would just call them up or write them or tell the brand inspector, who knew that they had too many cattle. The other people would know about it, and instead of trying to truck them over, the original owners might sell them locally or they might sell them to the ranch that already had them. You couldn't sell anything in Wyoming unless it was inspected by the brand inspector when it was sold, so it was very hard to sell anyone else's brand unless you sold a cow without the brand inspector's knowing it, and that's against the law.

That law was very seldom broken. I mean, there used to be a story I heard around Jackson's Hole at the time that it was a helluva lot safer to shoot a man than it was to steal a cow. You got more years in Rawlins for rustling a cow than you did for killing a man. It was the law of the land, enforced if need be by bullets or a long time in the state penitentiary.

***

A good friend of mine once got in big trouble for mistaking elk for cattle. After Geraldine Lucas's climb in 1924, I barely had enough time to get some itchy hay in my underwear before Bill Lucas was driving me back into Jackson to meet with Mr. Owen and to plan his second attempt on the peak. Ike Powell was to pack us up on the treacherous trails through Death Canyon to the base of the Middle Teton, where we would establish our camp. After another of Mrs. Crabtree's delicious breakfasts, Mr. Owen sent me over to the livery stable to collect Ike, who had bunked there for the night with his saddle horse.

When I saw Ike I was stunned by his appearance. One eye was almost swollen shut and his face was covered with bruises. He was busy wiping away blood that was dripping from his swollen nose. At first, I thought he had been in the saloon the night before and had gotten into a brawl. But I also knew that, although Ike was no teetotaler, he was not much more than a social drinker.

"What the hell happened to you?" I blurted out. "Somebody beat you up?"

"Forget about it," Ike said. "It's a personal thing."

"It may be personal," I said, "but it looks like somebody beat you up."

"It was the game warden," he said.

"I thought the game wardens arrested you," I said. "I didn't know they enforced the law by beating up people."

"We've had a disagreement for a long time," Ike said. "He's taken offense to a few things I've said about the elk. It isn't that important, and I don't know why he's so damn concerned about it. But let's drop it. I don't want our feud to get all over the country."

"What kind of a feud?" I asked, but he said no more. After washing his face, he took a full breath and managed a brave smile. "Let's go talk to Mr. Owen about the trip," he said. Mr. Owen was prudent enough not to inquire about Ike's injuries, perhaps assuming as I did that Ike had been in a saloon fight, a not-uncommon event in Jackson's Hole.

Later I asked Ike again about his fight with the game warden. He told me that during the winter he had fed some elk on the little ranch he had north of Jackson and now, for the summer, he kept them fenced in while they gave birth to their calves. He was either going to kill and eat them during hunting season or raise some more for the next year.

He said there was no law against what he was doing, but the game warden just didn't think he should be doing it. So instead of arresting him, he beat him up. I was incensed at this story, because Ike had one leg that was shorter than the other and although he could get around and climb all right, he was probably at a disadvantage during a fight. I thought it was an unfair way to settle a disagreement. I didn't know at that time that my sense of fairness would be more dangerous to me in Jackson's Hole than my climbing mountains.

***

In the early days of Jackson's Hole, even as late as the time I started ranching in the middle thirties, it was common practice for ranchers to kill as many deer, elk, and moose as they needed for their winter supply. Without refrigeration the only way they had to keep the meat was to wait until the weather was cold enough that it would freeze on its own, which usually meant after hunting season. That meat lasted until March or April. We got our winter supply from the last elk that moved through. At that time of the year the game wardens went to visit relatives or played cards in the local saloons.

The year I owned Ramshorn, which is now the Teton Science Center, we killed a number of elk and one moose. We canned a lot of it, we made jerky out of some of it, and we took the large parts, like the hindquarters and the frontquarters and loins, or sometimes the whole carcass with the skin left on it, out to the barn and hung it on the north side of the shed till it froze. Then we covered it with hay, top and bottom. We even buried some under the haystacks. That would remain frozen all winter and stay frozen practically until the snow was melted in the spring.

Of course, when we did kill these elk we didn't do it with a lot of flair. We did it as inconspicuously as we could, because it was still against the law, even though we knew the game wardens were not looking for us. One day, on a hill just south of the Ramshorn where we had our cabin, there were some cow elk grazing up about halfway down the hill. They hadn't gone on down to the feed grounds; they were still pawing in the snow and could paw off enough snow to get to the grass. That was a wonderful way to eat, because the cured grass and weeds underneath the snow, even though it wasn't green anymore, were still good nourishment.

I thought maybe I wouldn't need a gun, and wouldn't need to have the neighbors hear the shots. I would spear this elk. So I got a long piece of lodgepole pine, a small tree, and whittled it down. I had a big, big, long butcher knife, which was very sharp, and I wired it onto the end of my pole like a spear.

I went on my skis around back of this hill and came over the top. In theory, I was going to schuss down on this elk. There was one cow there that was very dark-colored, which generally meant it was a dry cow, that it had lost its calf during the spring. We looked for this type of dry cows to kill in the fall, because they were generally fatter and were in much better shape than the cows that had nursed calves all summer.

So I picked this one out and I started down the hill toward her. She saw me coming and she didn't wait to be stabbed. She took a look at me and she started to run up the hill toward me. I had to try a sudden telemark with my spear and I fell down. But I didn't lose the skis. So I got up and I was going faster and faster and faster down the hill with this elk running in back of me. I gained speed faster than she could run and escaped back to the ranch.

I was in such disrepute from my brother and a couple of cowboys for trying this crazy thing. "By God, if those elk get to you, all it takes is a couple of those sharp hooves and you've had it." As far as I know, that spear is still up there above the ranch. It was lost under six feet of snow in the winter, and I never bothered to go look for it.

***

My brother and I were out sort of exploring once, maybe looking for some good logs for building. My brother had a rifle with him, but he only had a little ammunition. We saw this spike elk, which was very good meat. It was a yearling. They have a horn but generally it's just a spike shaped like a V. They're young and tender and fat and they're not yet trying to chase the big bulls away from the herd.

So he shot it. We had some horses along, so we were just going to throw it over the top of the saddle and bring it home that way and walk home; we weren't very far out. It ran and he shot at it again — he'd hit it — and he shot two or three times more and we followed it to where it sort of went over a bank. There it was, wounded, lying just behind a great big tree. We thought we shouldn't disturb it, because lots of times they lie down like that and they never get back up. But if you disturb them they might run again.

But we didn't have any more ammunition and we could see its tail sticking out from behind this tree. My brother had a hunting knife with a blade on it about six inches long. Anyway, I borrowed it and I sneaked up and got right behind the tree. The elk didn't get up, so I got all ready. Luckily, it was on the side of the tree where I could jump around with my right hand on the outside, so I was ready to stab him.

I jumped around the tree, and he was still well enough to jump up. I swung the knife at him and stuck it in his back. He took off. He was pretty badly wounded, so I rushed after him. He came to a shelf that went down to the river, and when he went over the bank I grabbed him. I fell down and he fell down and we both rolled down this bank. When we got to the bottom I pulled out the knife and cut his throat.

That was a story my brother used to tell with elaboration, and I always hated to tell it because it sounded like such a heroic thing — you know, killing an elk with your bare hands and all that crap. The elk would have probably died in five minutes anyway.

Once I was on this talk show — I've forgotten what the host's name was but he was an Englishman, very popular in those days. There were a couple of other guys on this talk show too who had had all sorts of adventures. The first question he asked me was, "I hear that you ran down and killed a bull elk with a pocketknife in Jackson's Hole. I wish you'd tell the people about that."

Well, what was I going to do? God, I was so embarrassed. So I told them and I elaborated a little bit.

***

I remember talking to one game warden about his early experiences trying to enforce the hunting laws. He told me about going down to the southern part of Jackson's Hole and out to the Snake River Canyon in an attempt to stop poaching in Afton, Alpine, and Swan valleys. Those people figured since they helped feed the game during the winter, they were entitled to shoot what they needed for themselves. This game warden decided to have a showdown with them, even at the risk of his own life. He planned that the first man he arrested would be a man of some standing in the community, so he arrested a Mormon bishop. He made the charges stick, and that was the unofficial beginning of game law and order in that country.

The people living on the Idaho side went up and hunted in the Tetons all the time, even crossing the state border into Wyoming. The great hunting always took place before the haying and harvesting season. Ranchers would go up there to get deer, elk, and moose to feed their harvesting crews. In those days, there was a lot of hand work in harvesting, which required a big crew — and big crews needed a lot of meat. After the game wardens started cracking down, the ranchers had to devise ways to get the meat they needed, while avoiding the wardens. That is when the thing with the packhorses started.

The ranchers would go up near the ridge of the mountains, over the state line into Wyoming, and shoot their game. Then they loaded the meat on their big packhorses that knew the way home. At dusk, they would turn the packhorses loose to make their way back to the barn. The ranchers would wash all traces of the meat off themselves and ride "clean" down the trail back to their ranches in Idaho. They knew when they got home their packhorses would be standing outside the corral waiting to get in.

The packhorses were practically impossible for the game wardens to catch. Whenever they got close the horses would head off the trail through the timber and brush. What few Idaho wardens there were, were only interested in protecting the game in Idaho, so if the Wyoming wardens didn't catch them while they were still up on the Wyoming part of the mountain, the ranchers were home free.

***

Moose used to come down from the hills and they'd bother the cattle. The cattle are afraid of the moose, but the moose aren't afraid of humans. They don't run in the wintertime when we come around. They just stand there and watch you.

This one moose was being a real nuisance. He was eating the cows' hay and I don't know why, but I just picked up a big clod of frozen dung about the same weight as a baseball. I wound up and threw it at him and hit him right in the eye. Boy, did he come after me.

The snow was all packed down in the feeding lot and kind of icy. I started running and I heard him coming and there was a quaking aspen tree up ahead. I took ahold of that quaking aspen tree and swung around and he went sliding by. He turned around and charged me again, and I swung around another quaking aspen tree. He got off a ways, shook his head, and took off for the timber. But I was a Spanish moose-fighter for two charges.

CHAPTER FIVE

LIFE IN
THE HOLE

"Of all places in the Rocky Mountains that I know, it is the most beautiful, and, as it lies too high for man to build and prosper in, its trees and waters should be kept from man's irresponsible destruction."
— *Owen Wister, 1892*

Jackson's Hole was a terrific place to learn about people and human nature. Perhaps because of its isolation, it was a place where many people thought they could escape the realities of life. I certainly couldn't blame them. To me the realities of life were much less complex in Jackson's Hole than in the big cities.

If a person had a farm or a ranch or worked at the many jobs available in the valley, it didn't cost much to live. Most people were not specialists of any one trade or skill, but jacks of all trades.

The people of Jackson's Hole worked in the hayfields, and branded and herded cattle and watched over the herds while they were in their summer grazing grounds. They were carpenters and bartenders, and in the summer some worked as gamblers in the saloons or in some way taking care of the dudes. There were teachers and the people who drove sleds full of kids from Mormon Row to the school at Kelly in the winter. It was a seasonal way to live. Hunting was seasonal, fishing was seasonal, putting up the hay and gathering firewood were seasonal, and the dude wrangling was seasonal.

One of the most seasonal occupations was trapping. Some trappers made enough money in the wintertime to get along all year, but most of them worked other jobs in the summer. I got acquainted with one trapper who trapped in the Wind Rivers where there was good martin country. Good martin trapping depended on where a trapper found the highest squirrel population. I think that particular squirrel in the Wind Rivers was called the Wind River pine squirrel.

Martin skins were extremely salable in those days because of a fad that had developed among wealthy women. They would wear two full martin hides, tails and all, around their necks and over their shoulders. This was an "in" thing in those days. I can remember seeing women wearing those things so the head of one martin was biting into the tail of another, making a circle around their necks.

***

I never really made the town of Jackson my headquarters. When I returned to Jackson's Hole in 1925, a few people were camped down at the Jenny Lake campground, and that's where I set up. It was small enough that everybody was in hollering distance of everybody else. There were evenings around the campfire when stories were told, and people asked if I knew their friends the Lewises from St. Louis. Even in those days some of the older people camping there would show pictures of their grandchildren.

The Johnsons opened a little restaurant, a tent restaurant. Mrs. Johnson had a reputation in the valley for camp cooking equal to Mrs. Crabtree's reputation in Jackson. Homer Richards, who had homesteaded around Jenny Lake and whose property even took in some of the edges of Jenny Lake, was a big promoter of tourism and supported the trail-building program that was going on at the time. He also made a living by having a little barber shop and cutting the cowboys' hair.

There was also a little store that supplied groceries and knickknacks for the tourists, locals, and a handful of dude ranches that were close to Jenny Lake so people didn't have to make the twenty-mile trip to Jackson. It was a very comfortable community.

Perhaps the most important feature of the Jenny Lake community was the new dance hall, where once or twice a week, at least every Saturday night, the jazz orchestra played the great

Paul before a dip in Leigh Lake 1930. (Glenn Exum Collection)

dance tunes of the time. Tourists, dudes, and the local population mingled together without inhibition or class distinction and enjoyed the revelry. No cowboy in Jackson's Hole had any inhibitions about asking a lady from Philadelphia to dance.

Always outside, discreetly parked behind some bushes, was a Buick. Out of the back end of this car were delivered pints or half pints of moonshine from one of Jackson's Hole's best stills. These illegal stills not only had liquor for the various dances and other social meetings, but supplied the saloons in Jackson itself. Prohibition was never part of Jackson's Hole. Starting the first day I set foot in Jackson, and all during the years of prohibition, I could always get a drink over the bar.

For shelter, I had secured a small wall tent, as we called it in those days. It was canvas with a peaked roof and four straight sides. It was the type of small tent that people strapped on their front fenders when they went camping in the mountains. Many people coming from Yellowstone had their tents strapped on in this way. The floor of my tent was covered with pine needles, and a small campfire could be built outside for cooking.

There were a lot of adventurous young people coming through Jenny Lake. There were people like Gustav and Theodore Koven — Gus and Ted — two athletic-looking men who showed up at my camp in the trees at Jenny Lake in 1931. Their father had immigrated from Germany and had started a successful foundry business in New Jersey. During World War I, their father's company had helped manufacture some of the first submarines for our navy.

When they came to the Tetons, they had some climbing experience but were looking for a real climb. They said they wanted to hire me as a guide, and they were direct in their approach. I told them Mount Owen had been climbed only once before and asked them if they wanted to try it. They liked the idea.

Climbing with the Kovens was enjoyable because they shared my philosophy about going up a mountain. It wasn't just a hell-bent trip to get to the top to take a picture back to an office in New York. It was something to appreciate. Unless weather threatened, it should be a leisurely event. The new route we pioneered up Mount Owen I eventually named the Koven Route.

Later that summer, I climbed extensively with the Kovens in the Wind Rivers. Unfortunately, an accident on Mount McKinley in 1932 brought Ted Koven's climbing career, which had begun so brilliantly, to a tragic end. He died while on a cosmic-ray research expedition with Allen Carpe. Their bodies were never retrieved from the crevasses of the Muldrow Glacier.

We got people like that, but we also got just regular campers who came through on their way to Yellowstone and had a little time and had never thought about climbing mountains. We would talk to them and tell them about what we were doing. They'd become interested, and we'd get them to go on a climb. We tried to sell the idea to everyone who camped there, that is, if they had the physical capability of climbing with us. We'd approach them all. We assisted in giving lectures there in the evening, so we became known that way, and the rangers at Jenny Lake were all for us. If people were looking for something to do, the rangers might even suggest going to see the guides and climbing one of the mountains.

The summer rangers had a new little museum and information cabin there. And they were camped in the campgrounds. They lived there in the campgrounds in tents and so forth. Phil Smith, a climbing ranger and one of my part-time guides, was there with his family, so they became part of the community. The park headquarters was down the road several miles. That's where all the formal business and paperwork was done, and if any of those park people came up to Jenny Lake to mix with the tourists, it was only on special occasions. They weren't there every day.

In the early days I threw in with Olaf Moller and Archie Teater, two free-spirited artists plying their trade amid the beautiful scenery of Jackson's Hole and the Tetons. Archie was a self-taught painter whose paintings I loved. They were rugged and realistic, and I used to say Archie painted mountains I could climb. I accompanied Olaf on many occasions to watch him paint the Tetons and to help him select some extraordinary views.

Archie and Olaf moved to the Jenny Lake campground because it was a good location to sell their paintings. It became a ritual for us. When tourists arrived there in the afternoon, we'd greet them and ask them where they were from and various other questions. Then we would invite them to come over and look at the paintings that Olaf and Archie had leaning up against pine trees. I would talk to them about the adventure of climbing the Grand Teton or going up onto the glacier or other types of activities with, of course, a paid guide who could bring them safely back from such expeditions.

The three of us lived together in a communal fashion. If rations got low, the one with the money went to the store to buy more food. If they sold a painting, we ate. If I made a climb, we ate. There was never any misunderstanding or argument as to who was furnishing the money.

***

Even after I had firmly established myself as the sole concessionaire in Teton National Park, I returned to live at Jenny Lake. I wasn't making a lot of money, but that was a time when a cup of coffee was a nickel, a hamburger was fifteen cents, and you could get a full meal for forty cents. I'll never forget the first time I had to pay a dollar for a steak. I thought the world was coming to an end. If we were busy, guiding was better than a job haying, or a job as a working man. Besides that, I was happy, I had a certain amount of prestige, I met many interesting people, and it was fun. It was work that was fun.

From the old canvas-tent store, I purchased a fine tepee that was about twenty- to twenty-five feet across at the bottom and rose up about twenty-five feet. For the tepee poles I used lodge-pole pine that, when it's thick, grows very straight. That's what the Indians made their tepee poles out of. The tent was also patterned after the old Indian tepees, with a skirt along the bottom to protect against the wind. When we built a fire in the middle, the smoke rose through the opening at the top where all the tepee poles were fastened together. Depending on which way the wind was blowing, a shield at the top of the tepee could be positioned using strings so the wind blew the smoke away instead of back down into the tent.

I was the only one at Jenny Lake who had a tepee, and it was a rather expensive investment at the time. But it worked out very well for me. If anyone was inquiring around the camp about getting a guide for mountain climbing, all people had to say was, "He lives in that tepee up at Jenny Lake." So everybody knew where to find me.

Of course, some dudes and tourists who came through there thought since there was a tepee, there had to be Indians. People would just walk into our tent asking to see the Indians.

My wife was living with me then, and we were meeting some interesting people who came through Jenny Lake, some who stayed quite a while. The Stagners started showing up. *Wow!* They were some of the first acrobatic climbers I knew. They weren't particularly interested in climbing mountains; they were interested in climbing hard chimneys or cracks. The Stagners were from the Chicago Mountaineering Club and had been circus performers, maybe tightrope walkers or the men on the flying trapeze, but they were the first sport climbers I knew. They were impressive, and I learned some techniques from watching them. But these were mostly techniques we didn't need to use on our climbs.

Bob Carmichael was working as a fishing guide and was living next to us. If it was raining, we cooked in the tepee, but most of the time we cooked outside and often shared meals with our neighbors. There was a friendly ranger working for the park at that time named Alan Cameron, the first ranger besides Smith and the geologist Fritiof Fryxell, who were temporary rangers, to do a little climbing. He promoted our climbing and also promoted our entertainment of the growing number of people camping at Jenny Lake.

The park built a little amphitheater near the ranger station, where rangers could give lectures and people could be entertained in the evening. When I wasn't camping at timberline with a client, lots of times I gave lectures there on mountaineering. It was very helpful to my business. Many times people who were camped there would come up after the lecture and would want to climb the Grand Teton or some other mountain or at least go to our daily climbing school at Hidden Falls.

Hidden Falls was a couple of miles walk on the trail around the lake from the campground, but there was a boat concession then, a fella with a couple of motorboats that would hold three to five people at a time. We generally took our group across on the motorboat, which was inexpensive since he gave us a special rate. He would pick us up at a certain time in the afternoon.

There was also a horse concession there at the time. One ride was around Jenny Lake, up above Hidden Falls, and up Cascade Canyon, where there was a beautiful view of the north slopes of Mount Owen and Teewinot. However, as the horse business improved, there were some problems. The horses had a tendency to fill up on hay but not eliminate it until they got out on the trail. In the summertime, the smell of manure mixed with the fine dust kicked up by the horses. When a hiker breathed in that combination it had a tendency to make his supper taste like horse manure. We called this the barnyard syndrome.

CHAPTER SIX

BARON EXUM

"Any old woman can climb that."
— *The wind to Glenn Exum*

In 1930, I had already been given the guiding concession in the park and had the practice of climbing there well established. I was using Phil Smith and Floyd Wilson as assistant guides. Then I met Glenn Exum. We quickly became friends, possibly because we had so much in common. We were both from Idaho and both had rather rough backgrounds. We seemed to understand each other without conversation. Glenn was part of an orchestra, and the first time I heard him play in downtown Jackson I was amazed by his dexterity. He sounded like some of the best players in the big bands of that time.

Glenn also was a natural climber. He possessed strength, balance, and agility, some prerequisites for being a good mountaineer. He also had, in my opinion, a guide's personality. One overlooked skill of a good guide, which Glenn possessed, was an ability to keep the trip fun and interesting for the clients in ways other than just the climbing itself.

By 1931 I had hired Glenn as my assistant. He was also playing in the orchestra in the local saloons and in the dance hall at Jenny Lake. He was a great asset to me because he would introduce me to various gals I could dance with, both local and dude girls, who admired his good looks and his wielding of a wicked sax. I thought it was only fair that I do something for him in return. We had made a couple of climbs together the year before, but now I wanted to make him a full-fledged guide. He could climb during the week and help me on some Teton trips even though he was playing most of the weekends.

Paul (left) and Glenn Exum, after Paul had taken Glenn on his first climb, the Owen Route of the Grand Teton, August 1930. (Glenn Exum Collection)

On July 15, I was scheduled to guide a couple from Ohio up the Grand Teton. They had just returned from climbing in Austria. I was anxious to climb with them because I thought they might be able to answer my many questions about European guiding techniques, the sort of equipment European guides used, and how they handled their clients. Glenn had a couple of nights off, so I suggested he come along.

Having Glenn on the trip gave me a wonderful opportunity to do two things: give Glenn some actual guiding experience with clients and also do some exploring and experimenting. The night before we left I discussed my plan with Glenn, and he was enthusiastic about it. Years before, I had seen a ledge on the south side of the Grand Teton that looked like it offered some potential as a climbable route. Up to that time, only two routes had been used to climb the Grand, the Owen Route and the East Ridge Route, pioneered in 1929 by Bob Underhill, a noted climber from the American Alpine Club, and Kenneth Henderson. I knew if my guiding service were to flourish, I would have to offer some variety in the climbs. Also, I needed a new challenge.

It was important for me to look at the route that particular day, because I got wind that another party, led by Underhill, was trying for a new route somewhere in that vicinity. I didn't think it was the route I was looking at, because it would have been extremely difficult to scale the vertical wall leading up to the ledge from the bottom of the mountain. But I didn't want to take any chances since I had studied the ledge for seven years. I wanted first crack at it.

I asked Glenn to explore the ledge. It started out about twenty feet wide but narrowed out to a point where I thought he could get around the corner to a ridge that wouldn't be visible from where I would be with the clients, but that I had viewed from the top of the Middle Teton. He left our party, crossed a gully, and as we climbed we watched him moving rapidly up the ledge. A short time later I saw that he had reached the end of the ledge and was peering around the corner. I yelled to him to hurry back and join us so he could tell me what was there and continue with us for the rest of our climb up the Owen Route.

Well, the wind was blowing that day, and Glenn yelled back something that I couldn't understand. What he was saying was that there was a wide gap that we couldn't see from where we were, separating the end of the ledge from a platform at the base of the ridge heading up the mountain. Glenn had already leaped across this gap, which dropped off one thousand feet. It would have meant certain death if he had fallen.

I never did measure Glenn's long jump, but when I first saw it I knew it was too far for me or anybody else to chance jumping. But Glenn had done it and now he couldn't get back. He was yelling to me that he would have to go on up to the top to get off the mountain, but I still couldn't hear what he was saying.

If Glenn needed any inspiration to complete his climb, he got it from the wind. I found out later that my calls to Glenn to come back were interpreted through the howling breeze by him as "Any old woman can climb that." Glenn thought this was a very unkind observation, considering his heroic leap over the chasm, which I don't think has been duplicated to this day, or at least I hope not.

Glenn said later that he was sitting comfortably on top waiting for me when he saw my bushy eyebrows blowing in the wind as I stuck my head up over the last cliff before the summit. It was a historic event and we all congratulated Glenn for pioneering the third route up to the top of the Grand Teton. To honor Glenn and to increase his prestige as a guide, I named the route the Exum Ridge.

But the day wasn't over yet. Glenn joined us for our descent down the Owen Route, and we made good progress to where we had parted earlier. I asked Glenn to take the couple down the rest of the way so I could have a look at the Exum Ridge. He said he could lead them down to timberline and put them on a trail, but from there he would have to leave them so as not to be late for his gig.

This was acceptable to the couple, so I raced up the ledge to where I got my first glance at the awful abyss that Glenn had leaped. I wanted no part of it. I did see that by climbing down into this gap a little ways, there were some handholds that I could reach by straddling my legs across the space. From there I could climb up to where Glenn had landed with his jump. It was wonderful scrambling up to the top of the Grand Teton after that.

The climb energized me so much that I raced down the mountain and caught my clients before they reached camp. It was the first time the Grand had been climbed twice in one day.

***

When the Dean of Windsor was in Jackson's Hole, Glenn came out to the Gray ranch and met him. Glenn talked about saving his money because he wanted to visit Europe sometime. I had been hired by Prentice Gray to guide the dean on walks and I talked to the dean about Glenn quite a bit. I told him Glenn might go to Europe and suggested maybe he could visit Windsor Castle for a short time. I think the dean sent Glenn an invitation.

Glenn arrived there and experienced what he told me was the most embarrassing moment of his life. Glenn was invited to many social gatherings, like the queen's garden parties, and at one of these parties he was introduced to Lady Goofus-Frazier, or somebody like that. Somebody with one of those double English names. Somebody with breeding that counted. In those days, you could be the most intelligent, productive person in the world, but you only got into certain circles with breeding, not by what you knew or what you did.

These people really did have what I would call class. They had certain definite types of behavior that nobody varied from. It was very predictable. This beautiful lady sat down at a table with Glenn, and they were having a refreshment of some kind. Glenn obviously was a little nervous. He saw something on the table and, subconsciously — I guess he would have done it at home — he just flipped it with his finger to get it off the table.

It was bird dung. So there he was with a big chunk of bird dung on the nail of his flip finger. Well, Lady Frazier didn't stop talking; she didn't blink an eye; she didn't make one unusual movement. She took Glenn's hand and took her napkin, or whatever they called those in England, and wiped off his finger as if nothing had happened. That was the best demonstration I've ever heard of real English class.

Glenn Exum (left), Barbara Gray, and Paul taken in 1932 before climbing Nez Pierce. Notes of interest: Barbara Gray was the first woman to climb Nez Pierce. She was also the daughter of Prentice Gray, who was responsible for introducing Paul to the Dean of Windsor. (Glenn Exum Collection)

***

When Glenn got back to New York he stayed with Gus Koven. Gus was heading out to Jackson's Hole and he had friends out there from San Francisco who were super, super, super rich, perhaps the Levi Strauss people. They had invited Gus to come to their ranch, and on the way out he called them and said he was bringing along "Baron" Exum.

Well, they said, of course, he's welcome too. "Baron" Exum was impressive to even the richest San Franciscans. They spruced up everything and got some specially made clothes for the maid, a local gal from Jackson. They had everything all fixed up for an afternoon arrival of the European aristocracy. The hour had been set by the latest telephone call. So here Glenn and Gus arrived at this ranch in front of the Tetons along the Snake River. It was a place that was never for sale, not even to the Rockefellers. Gus's friends didn't need the money.

The whole place was all laid out for Baron Exum. And Exum should have been an actor. He was terrifically handsome, as was his brother. As a matter of fact, his brother did go to Hollywood and was doing quite well until one day he became ill and died shortly after from spinal meningitis. With Glenn's musical ability and good looks I think he really missed his calling. I think he would have been a star in Hollywood.

But in his role as Baron Exum he was putting on a terrific act. Then the maid came in with more hors d'oeuvres, put down the plate, walked over to Glenn, and hugged him. "Well, hello Glenn," she said. "When did you get back?" Glenn never did tell me how he got out of that one.

CHAPTER SEVEN

OF FISH
AND BEARS

"The river just showed through the trees. There were plenty of days coming when he could fish the swamp."
— *Ernest Hemingway, "Big Two-Hearted River"*

Soon after the famous fisherman Bob Carmichael came to the Tetons, I came into camp one night with a string of fish that I had caught in the Snake River. He asked me where I had caught the fish, and as we talked I was impressed with his terrific background and his unbelievable knowledge of streams and trout.

I knew that he was a fly fisherman and I told him I had tried fly-fishing too, but I didn't have the right equipment. "Anyway, the way I fish I can catch the big ones," I said. "With flies you only catch the little ones."

"You think so?" he said. We almost immediately became friends because he was very knowledgeable about world affairs and politics. I soon learned that he had been a well-known reporter for one of the big press outfits and had spent quite a bit of his life in Washington, D.C. He had come to Jackson's Hole with the hope of doing more fishing than drinking, which, he told me, was a secondary occupation for many people in the newspaper business.

He could catch fish with dry flies quicker and bigger than I could with worms or minnows or live bait or even dynamite. I was amazed at what he could do with dry flies. A wet fly can be pulled through the water and will fool a fish into thinking it is some sort of water bug swimming in the water or perhaps a small minnow. But a dry fly, which floats on the water, has to be cast just right so it looks like a moth or insect committing suicide. It has to drop down gently onto the water and can't slap it.

Bob wouldn't do much casting. He would walk along the river and see where a trout was rising. He could tell by the way it broke the surface how big it was. Because it was competing for food, a little trout would come up to the surface very fast and grab an insect, sometimes so fast it would extend out of the water and flop down. Bob would know that was a little fish. A big trout would come to the surface and its nose would barely be visible as it glupped the insect in. Bob would go along until he saw where one was glupping and then he would cast.

The big fish are smart and most times won't be fooled more than once, so Bob's thing was to get them on the first cast. He put his fly in the air and stayed out of sight until one rose. By the time it had gone back under, Bob's fly would commit suicide within inches of where the trout had risen. When the trout grabbed his fly he would hook it gently. With a leader that only tested three pounds, which is very fine so that it looks like the fly isn't attached to anything, Bob would land a four-pound trout. I considered his fishing an art.

When Bob's fishing companion left to go back to civilization I tried to convince Bob to stay. "Gosh, there's a future for you in this country," I said. "I'll introduce you to the people from the dude ranches and you can make some money here. There's nobody that ever came into this country that fishes like you do."

That may not have been true, but Bob was considered one of the best fly fishermen in the United States. Other trout fishermen later told me that he was the best river man or stream man, which meant that he may not have taken first in fly-casting tournaments, but he was one of the best in the business when it came to river techniques.

He used to have me stand seventy to seventy-five feet or more away from him and he could fly cast — not with a hook on (but I would have trusted him with a hook) — and take a cigarette out of my mouth. The rangers saw this and they had us come down at night to the little amphitheater near the ranger station and Bob would demonstrate his technique. He insisted that the cigarette be lit, because that made it more dramatic.

My attempt at smoking in my youth was disastrous, because my tonsils had been jerked out by wires as they did in those days and it had left some scars. Every time I smoked I got a sore throat, which is perhaps why I didn't smoke. But everyone had to smoke in those days to be a man, because all the movie actors smoked. After Bob had taken the lit cigarette out of my mouth the rangers would come over and stamp it out to be sure it didn't start a forest fire. They didn't want the tourists to think that lit cigarettes could be thrown away.

I introduced Bob around some of the dude ranches, and immediately he was busy as a fishing guide in Jackson's Hole. He decided he could make a living there, so he came back the next summer. I introduced him to a schoolteacher who had made a climb to the top of the Grand Teton, and that blossomed into a romance and a marriage that ended up with her running the post office and him owning a fishing-tackle store and a guide service. In the fall when I wasn't climbing, he had taught me enough so that I could take out some of his dudes. I practiced and after a while I could have taken a cigarette out of somebody's mouth at fifty feet — but not at seventy-five.

***

I had an experience in the Teton marsh near the Snake River one day that became one of Phil Smith's funny stories, but wasn't very funny to me at the time. I was trying to catch some pan-size trout for a quick meal. A moose was feeding on the other side of this little beaver pond. He had his head in the water eating the growth at the bottom. When he rose up he would look at me with alarm and then start feeding again.

I had my fly already on and was fishing, and the next time he started to raise up I cast way out toward him. Unfortunately, I hooked him in the ear. I didn't know whether to try and reel him in or not and I knew I couldn't hold him if he took off. He just looked at me with a steady eye, and I was the first one to blink. He started splashing across the swamp toward me in a determined way, and I took off dragging the line behind me, still holding on to my fishing rod. Once I got through the bushes he quit following me. I think the fly is still stuck in his ear. Maybe some hunter will find it this fall.

"You see this little fly here? This is one I invented. I call it the Whitcraft fly, and it's one of the best in this valley. I named it after Superintendent Whitcraft, who I taught to fish with flies. The tourists don't like these things. They're not bright-colored and they're small. But in order to make a living I've got to sell stuff that looks good to the tourists, not stuff that looks good to the trout."

There is another Bob Carmichael story that doesn't have to do with fish. I had gone to a dance; I guess Glenn Exum was playing someplace so I'd gone to town. This was late in the fall, a frosty night, and when I got back home that night the ground was covered with frost. When I rode up to our campsite, the sound of our car frightened away a bear that had been hanging around.

Carmichael had stayed home and was sleeping when he heard something rattling around outside, so he got up with just his underwear on and climbed out of his tent. The noise turned out to be a bear, so he naturally threw a stick at it. The next thing he knew he was up a tree and the bear was clawing at the bark of the tree. The bear had a rather large cub with her and she would go off to check her cub, but the moment he made any noise to start down from the tree the bear would come running back.

When we got back real late that night he was in the first stages of hypothermia. He'd been up there a few hours in just his underwear. I'm not a bear psychologist; I don't know exactly what the bear was thinking. But she was thinking clearly enough that he wasn't going to get down out of that tree. The next day we took Carmichael down to the hospital. He got some medicine, but he wasn't fishing for several days after that.

**

One of the biggest problems in Grand Teton National Park, and one that still exists today, was tourists feeding the bears, or "bars," as we called them. Bears had learned that tourists had food. We soon learned that once a bear associated people with food, they would wander brazenly into camps. They were more difficult to break of this habit than a person on drugs, and there were no psychologists to cure bears of associating campers with good food.

Bears looking for food was also a great problem at the horse camps. Horses are naturally afraid of bears, and when a bear came down around the tents to where the cowboys slept and near the corrals, the horses would become frantic, sometimes breaking through the corrals and injuring themselves.

Once, some cowboys got an idea that they were going to fix the bear. They bought their horseshoes in large amounts, which were delivered in a small oak barrel. The cowboys really wanted to get even with the bear, so they drove some spikes slanting downward through the sides of the barrel. They put the barrel out in the open and poured a can of honey in the bottom, knowing that the bear could not resist sticking his head in the barrel to get the honey. Then the nails slanting down in the barrel would prevent the barrel from coming off the bear's head. That would teach the bear a lesson.

It certainly did. That night a big black bear was enjoying the honey, which evidently is a bear delicacy, and it found it couldn't get its head out of the barrel. The bear started to run but couldn't see where it was going. After it ran straight into the cowboy-sleeping tent, clawing through both sides, the cowboys were wide awake. Of course, it was illegal to get out the old family 30-30 and eliminate bears the cowboy way, but something had to be done about "them thar bars."

***

I have some bear and fishing stories of my own. Bob liked one of my fishing stories so much I heard him telling it to the dudes. I learned to climb on the walls of the Snake River Canyon, since our home in Twin Falls was right near the edge of the canyon walls. As a matter of fact, we may have owned the land where years and years later Evel Knievel tried to jump the Snake River on his motorcycle. But luckily he had a parachute, so he landed down in the water near where my fish story begins.

One day I was fishing at a place called Pillar Falls. That was as high as the big sturgeon could get up the river in those days. Perhaps they don't get up that high anymore because of the dams, but back then they did. In the hardware store in Twin Falls they had one mounted on the wall, and the sign said it weighed sixteen hundred pounds.

All I knew then about the sturgeon was that they were there. I had seen my four older brothers and some neighbors put a cable across the Snake River to catch them. Using a boat they hung some big hooks baited with liver wrapped in cheesecloth from that cable. When a sturgeon was hooked, my brothers unhooked the cable on one side and attempted to pull in the fish, and these were pretty good-sized fish. Since we had no refrigerators in those days, the sturgeon was carried up to the top of the canyon in pieces and all the neighbors took some so it was eaten before it spoiled.

Pillar Falls had some big round holes worn in the rock where the water went around and around at the base of the falls. At the time, I was after some trout or whitefish, but as I was fishing I saw this big sturgeon come up through the foam and go down again. Every once in a while it would come up through the foam, where the water was whirling, and go down again. Well, that was enough for me.

I raced back up to our ranch and potato farm. My brothers immediately stopped all the farm work and notified one of the neighbors, and several adults came down to try to get the sturgeon. In this instance, my brothers used a long cane pole with eyelets. Rope ran through the eyelets with a big hook on the end that my brothers used to snag the sturgeon. After they hooked it, the fish bolted for the calm waters of the river below, and my brothers followed, trying to pull it in, which was only possible when it wanted to come in.

Suddenly, it evidently became confused and started right straight toward where we were pulling in the rope. It actually beached itself amid some boulders. My second oldest brother Louie didn't want the sturgeon to escape, so he ran down to grab it and just as he did the sturgeon flipped his tail and broke Louie's leg. But the sturgeon never did get back in the water. Somebody hit it over the head with a rock three or four times. Before we could dress out the sturgeon, we had to run back up to the ranch and get a stretcher. We tied my brother onto the stretcher, and with some evacuation skills acquired that day we managed to get him up the walls of the canyon and to the doctor in Twin Falls.

Some of the gossip around was that the fish weighed eight hundred pounds, and even making allowance for windage I suppose it weighed five hundred to six hundred pounds. All the neighborhood had sturgeon for a couple of days. Of course, in those days we had never heard of caviar and if there were any eggs they were discarded with the guts.

***

The real bear story maybe I shouldn't tell, but I will anyway. One late summer or fall, I was doing some fish guiding for Bob Carmichael and collecting some logs for a cabin I was planning to build near Moose. The park service gave me the cabin that used to be the summer home of the photographer Hank Crandall, out on the sagebrush flat by Jenny Lake near the Gabbey homestead. It was on the edge of the woods. I'd been hunting up the Gros Ventre — of course, I had a license — and I shot a deer. I dressed the deer out in the forest, quartered it, and brought the meat back to our cabin in the park.

There was no law against that. I think the park service knew I had deer meat, but I didn't shoot the deer in the park; I had taken it legally and tagged it up in the Gros Ventre. My wife's mother was visiting us then, and whenever I left, the two girls complained that every time they would go out to get some wood there would be these bears lounging around outside our cabin. This was very frightening to my wife and mother-in-law.

Then the bears became bolder. We had sort of a back porch that was well protected. Of course, the bears could have broken in the door if they had wanted to, but they didn't seem to know where the door was. One night we heard them slapping and hitting the logs — even knocking out some of the chinking — because just inside the back porch the quarters of deer were hanging. Then I heard a racket right outside the bedroom where I was sleeping, so I got up to look out the window. I saw what I thought was a reflection of myself in the window glass. Then I realized that the window was open. I blinked first and then I heard the bear run off through the bushes.

That was the end of it. We either had to move out or we had to do something about the bears. It had become absolutely intolerable. We had a little bench about twenty-five yards from the house, and one morning I came out and here were three of them sitting on the bench, just sitting there looking at us. Well, I thought, they're ganging up on us, so I went in the house and got my old Craig rifle with a heavy bullet in it.

I aimed very carefully, pulled the trigger, and shot one right below the throat, which I knew would be fatal. But I also knew if I did that, the other bears would go back to the wilds. Of course, I had a license to shoot a bear, but not a license to shoot a bear in the park. I knew the chief ranger pretty well and I thought I'd go down and tell him what the situation was, but I just let it go for that day.

The next night we didn't see the bears, but a day later I went out there to see how the bear was. I had gone up there when I first shot it, after the other bears had run, and saw that it was dead. It had been able to run a little ways into the bushes. I was thinking of the possibility of skinning the bear, then sneakily putting the hide in the car and driving way up the Gros Ventre, maybe sleeping out overnight, and then tagging the bear with my official tag and driving it back as if I'd killed it up the Gros Ventre. That was even a little bit too much for my sneaky ways, but I thought that might be a good plan.

I'd heard if you killed a bear and left it, other bears would drag it away and bury it. I didn't know if this was an old wives' tale or not, but some of the old trappers said bears didn't like fresh meat; they liked meat with maggots in it. They would hide it until it became ripe.

When I went out there I looked all around, and there was no sign of the bear. Then I became worried. I thought maybe while I was away the park rangers had come up there and found it and had taken it away for evidence. I saw myself doing a term in the federal prison. I looked and looked and never could find hide nor hair of the bear. It's something I've always had a little guilty conscience about.

***

I was guiding some young people. I think some may have been local and I'm not sure if we were just going up the glacier or climbing. But anyway, we were camped up at Surprise Lake.

It had been a gorgeous night, no sign of any clouds, so we just put our sleeping bags out on the grass near the edge of the lake in the open. In the night, I heard a noise and woke up. One of the campers in his sleeping bag was yelling, "George, cut that out!" George was the name of one of the people in our group. He kept yelling, "George, cut that out, George!"

I was looking over there — it was sort of a moonlit night — and I could see it was a bear rolling this guy around. Finally, he poked his head out of the sleeping bag and saw the bear hovering over him, and I swear he moved like one of those inchworms: He didn't get out of his sleeping bag, just inchwormed away from the bear, and the bear ran off in the woods. That was one of the most humorous sightings I ever had of a bear, and after that we called the camper's friend Bear George.

We had no fear of wild bears in the early days. The bears were frightened of human beings. I suppose a bear with cubs might attack you, but most of the incidents in Yellowstone were associated with food. One of the main attractions of going to Yellowstone in those days was to feed the bears. You would see the cars lined up and even the rangers would tell you where you could go see the bears. Lots of times there were dozens of cars stopped along the road, each one of them feeding the bears.

Some people would get out of their cars, and, of course, a lot of people got minor injuries. I'll never forget the time that I drove some dudes who wanted to see Yellowstone up to the park. They wanted to feed the bears and they were taking pictures out the window. A fella with a New Jersey license plate drove up, and there was a big old fat sow bear there waiting to eat. He threw a piece of candy to her, and she gobbled it up and then moved over toward his window. He put his hand out and dropped one practically into her mouth.

After she ate that she squatted down by the window like a calm dog. I was watching him and I thought, my God, that fella's taking an awful chance, but I didn't want to say anything. The next time, the bear was down on her haunches, and he took a piece of candy and held it out the window and said, "Up, up, up."

The bear didn't actually lick it out of his hand — I think he dropped it when the bear raised up her snout with her nose practically touching his hand. He reached over to get another piece of candy and I yelled at the top of my voice, "Please, don't do that again. Don't do that again!"

"Why not?" he asked.

"Well, sometimes these bears can't distinguish between your hand and what's in it," I said. "If she grabs your hand, you're coming right out through that window, glass or no glass."

He was convinced and he just threw the food out through a crack in the top of the window after that.

***

The next big show we had up there then was in the evening when they fed the bears. And they were feeding grizzlies. We went to this little sort of a stadium with plank seats to sit and watch the bears. There was a steel fence all around the stadium, and we were let in through a gate. During the day, they brought garbage from the hotel and dropped it there in front of the pavilion.

When it started to get dark, here came the grizzly bears to eat the garbage. I think people were starting to be more aware, as I was, of a new wilderness ethic and the idea that bears in Yellowstone should be wild and get their own food. It was becoming a real nuisance, because the grizzlies were becoming dependent on the dumps for food. If park officials cut the bears off from this food supply, they weren't sure what would happen. They weren't sure that the grizzlies wouldn't start roaming around the camps.

This became a dilemma for the park service. They were afraid not to put the garbage out where the bears were accustomed to eating it, not knowing what would happen. There was an argument about whether they should cut down on the garbage gradually so that hopefully some of the bears would go back to the wild, or whether they should do it cold turkey. That became a controversy between what the park wanted to do and what some of the budding specialists, such as my friends John and Frank Craighead, wanted to do.

The Craigheads got real involved from a hard-boiled,

practical standpoint. They were far ahead in their knowledge of the grizzly bear and they argued with the park people, who had a lot of book learning but not as much practical experience with the bears as the Craigheads did.

I think the Craigheads were some of the first to say the real truth: that you can't have tourists and grizzlies together. There is never going to be a time when you can have ordinary tourists out hiking in grizzly bear country and expect all of them to come back alive. It's like Kipling said about the East and West, "Never the twain shall meet." The grizzly bears and the Homo sapiens are like the East and West: They're never going to meet.

Well, they might meet. But if they do, generally the grizzly bear wins, temporarily. He wins the original fight, and then we come with our modern weapons and the grizzly bear is no more a competitor against a rifle than the Indians were. One of the world's greatest philosophers, Chairman Mao, said, "Politics comes from the end of a gun."

***

One of my good Wyoming friends in the early days was a doctor who practiced over in the Riverton Valley, some one hundred miles east of Jackson's Hole. Doc Ashbaugh was a doctor who told people the truth. Somebody told me the story about going up to his office one day, when he heard a commotion in the back room. The doctor was yelling at this woman, "If you think I'm going to give you one of those phoney diets that you won't keep anyway, you're barking up the wrong tree. Now you get your fat ass out of here and go home and stop eating!"

He was an enthusiastic fisherman and hunter, and one day he called me up and told me he'd bought a new boat and wanted me to take him out on Jackson Lake fishing. He was going to tow the boat over with his new car. In those days, the V-8 had just come out, and he had a special V-8 built, all tuned up to go fast, because he liked to drive fast.

He told me about one time he was really letting it out, driving between Riverton and DuBois. He said he was hitting about eighty-five miles an hour and he went over a hill and right in front of him was a band of sheep.

Well, a band of sheep is one thousand sheep, and if they have lambs with them then it's about two thousand. He said the car drove over those sheep like it was going over a feather bed. It cost him a little, because he had to pay for the sheep even though he knew he had butchered them and the meat was saved.

He told me over the phone when he would meet me at my camp at Jenny Lake, and the time he told meant he was going to fly. When he arrived we shook hands, and I said, "I thought you were going to bring your new boat."

He looked back behind the car and said, "Well, the sonofabitch was on there when I left Riverton."

I got back in the car with him and we started back on the awful dirt road over Togwotee Pass. We found the boat wrapped around a tree down in a gully all broken to pieces. "I guess I'll have to buy another one," he said. We went river fishing that day.

Doc Ashbaugh wanted to go elk hunting one day and I agreed to take him. I knew a place where we could get some elk that was pretty close. We got up there just at daylight and heard an elk bugle. I bugled, and he bugled back. I had a cut-off garden hose that had a notch in it like the whistles we used to make out of the bark of willows. We would slide the bark right off a willow stick, which was very slick inside, and that left a hollow tube. Then we cut a notch in the tube and one side was jammed so the air would flow through it like a musical instrument.

The garden hose worked in just the same way. With my hand I controlled the air coming through it so I could get something like an elk sound, which is sort of like ooooeeeeooooo. Then I'd go ungh ungh, and when he got close I took a stick and hit it on a log. That caused the elk to rack the bushes with his antlers to ward off other bull elk, because he may have had a harem he was protecting. We could hear the elk's antlers when he did this, so we knew he was coming toward us.

We were up where we could look over a knoll into an open meadow. Boy, he came out of the timber sweating and steaming and grunting and there he was standing right there broadside in front of us — an absolutely perfect picture. The doctor shot, and the elk jumped and looked around, but he couldn't see us. So he sniffed the air to find out where the noise was coming from. The doctor had a chance at another broadside shot.

"You didn't get him," I said. "In fact, you missed him entirely. Maybe you can squeeze the trigger this time."

He did, and the elk jumped again and ran away. Just as Doc fired the second bullet, I noticed, over about twenty or thirty feet, there was a tree that had fallen down or been blown over. As it had blown over its roots pulled out of the ground and they were sticking straight up in the air. Just as he shot I saw a bunch of dust come off the roots. I didn't say anything because I knew his eyes were a little bad.

***

I have to go quite a ways ahead for this story. After I got back from World War II, a person from Riverton called me up and said they had a new irrigation project that was coming there. They were building a canal somewhere. It was going to be divided up into homestead lots. It would be irrigated ground and would be worth some money, they thought, and it was open for a drawing for GIs. I didn't think anything about it. I've seen gambling enough to know that the chances of winning something like that are very slim, but I put in my name.

I was the third name drawn. After two other people had made their pick I got my pick of one of the spots in the project, so I got a pretty good one. I broke it up and started to farm it in absentia. I didn't see a future in the guiding business at that time that would make me the kind of living I wanted. Even though I was away during the war, the concession was still mine because the law said when you left anything like that to go to war, when you came back you got your job back. Glenn did some guiding while I was away, but during the war people were restricted by gasoline and things like that, so business wasn't too good.

Anyway, out on my ranch a fella had some cows and a bull that jumped over a barbed-wire fence and hurt his penis in such a way that they knew that he might die, but certainly wouldn't be any good as a bull anymore. So they butchered him and this fella, Stu, cut off the end of the penis, which was swollen and cut. He was a homesteader out there, a Missourian, who was always, always telling stories and pulling practical jokes. We had a little community store for this project, and he went into the store and said he'd been to Casper and gone to one of those naughty houses and he said, "I think that I've got something."

He unzipped his pants and pulled out what remained of this bull. Of course, everybody was shocked and laughed. "Let's go to Riverton and have some fun," he said.

So we went to the drugstore in Riverton where a fella I knew worked. "Stu went up to Casper and was a little naughty in one of those houses they got up there and I think there's something wrong with him," I said. "He'll need some medicine. Would you take him in back and look at it?"

So he took him in back and Stu unzipped his pants and the druggist said, "Oh my God, you'd better take that over and show it to Doc Ashbaugh."

So here we all marched over to Doc's office. We were very serious and we went into his private office and we told the story again. "Well, let's have a look at it," Doc said. So Stu pulled this thing out and the doctor looked at it for a long time. His secretary's name was Gertrude. "Gertrude! Gertrude!" he said. "Come in here fast." When she came in he said, "He's been down to Casper to one of those houses. You see what can happen to men that do things like that." She ran out screaming and we all laughed.

"You goddamn bastards," he said. "Take that up and show it to the mayor and tell him we have a new disease in town."

Doc used to tell me funny stories about some of his patients. There were two gals — I guess they were widows who had moved in together to share expenses. They were a little ways out of town and sort of a bother. They would come in for the slightest things. One day one of them called him up emergency-like and said her friend needed a doctor, immediately. It wasn't unusual for him to make farm calls — that's why he liked fast cars. At least that was his excuse.

When he arrived one of the women met him at the door and led him to the bedroom and said, "There she is doctor. There she is, lying prostitute on the bed!"

CHAPTER EIGHT

DUDES

"The dudes were fair game. There were certain principles we did have, but the object was to get their money and send them home happy."
— *Paul Petzoldt*

One of my good friends in Jackson's Hole in the early days was a fella called Slim Bassett, a real southerner who had migrated to the area. He was a strong, well-coordinated man with legs certainly long enough to reach the ground. He had long arms that dangled further down than most people's and big hands. He seemed to be able to do everything. He was a great hunter, a horse packer, and a cabin builder.

One of his endeavors was setting up a shingle mill down below Wilson where there were trees of the size and type that were good for making shingles. He desperately needed help, so whenever he was running his shingle mill, if I wasn't busy, he would come and get me to stack shingles. It was my job to kneel next to a giant buzz saw with a log the length of a shingle and rotate the log while the saw went up and down making its cuts.

It was a dangerous saw that spun around with terrific velocity and, of course, had to be sharpened each evening for work the next morning. It could have cut me in two, or cut a hand off, or anything that touched it could have been separated from my body. It was like making continuous dangerous moves on a mountain. I didn't relax for one second, because any mistake I made there was permanent. Ordinary cowboys didn't like that kind of action.

Slim and I became great friends. Later when I bought the little ranch up on Ditch Creek he would bring his pack outfit and dudes up there and use my place as a headquarters for hunting.

From there he could go to a little mountain called Mount Leidy that in those days was teeming with elk, the type of elk with large antlers. Of course, most dude hunters were after a good head that they could mount and hang in their office or home. Because of the lack of refrigerated transportation, they practically never took any meat home with them back East.

Slim had a good reputation for getting these big-antlered elk. Every year he would take out the people who owned Maytag, the big factory that made the famous washing machines, where the repairman is sleeping all the time. They also owned large chunks of Colorado real estate. Slim had dudes like that who, I am sure, added to his financial profits. He paid me well for using my place, and anybody frying the elk steak and putting out a good substantial meal was always taken care of too.

One spring Slim sent a bear hunter up to my place. I had a person working full-time for me there who kept charge of the ranch and was also an excellent guide. Perhaps the only reasons George worked for me for the meager wages he received was because I gave him a permanent place to live and I tolerated his idiosyncracies. When he was supposed to take a party out, if they took him to Jackson or he needed to go to Jackson after some equipment, he might bring home a little moonshine and not sober up for a couple of days.

But George was a terrific bear hunter. Sometimes, if he knew a bear hunter was coming, he would buy an old horse for a few dollars, take it out in the hills, shoot it, and leave it there as bait. When the horse got a little ripe, that's the kind of meat the bear liked. If it had a few maggots crawling around in it, that was cordon bleu for the bear.

That year he had no horse to shoot, so he had to bait the place with bacon. He planned to leave the bacon out there for the bear and he and the bear hunter would go out right at daylight hoping to find the bear still eating the bacon. They would shoot the bear if it was large enough or suitable for the bear rug that the dude needed to prove his nimrod ability.

When the bear hunter arrived, George told him they needed some bacon and he let him know that it was the dude's responsibility to supply it. They went down to Jackson and came back pretty sober with three slabs of bacon and no extra bottles. The first morning that they went out after they had left the bacon for the bear, the bacon was gone. But there on the ground were bear tracks. By measuring the width and length of the tracks, George knew it was a good bear.

The next morning, George said, they had to get out a little earlier. So they did, and the bacon was gone, and there were more tracks. Next, George said they had to go up there just before dark. Maybe the bear was coming in the evening. So they did, and, by God, the bacon was gone again.

They went to town, got three more slabs of bacon, and put one out that night. The next morning there was the bear. The bear hunter shot it with one shot right through the heart and was very happy. He had had a wonderful time and he gave George a big tip and tipped anyone else who was around. He left a very, very happy hunter.

The day after he left, George came in the house carrying some slabs of bacon and went out again. When he came back he had some more slabs of bacon. "I believe these five slabs of bacon will last us all winter," he said. He had an old bear claw he used to make tracks while he grabbed the bacon.

This was not an evil for the locals. The dudes were fair game. There were certain principles we did have, but the object was to get their money and send them home happy. You couldn't get their money and make them mad. You had to send them home happy.

***

People who had been hunting before with Slim insisted on having George as a guide because he had a sixth sense that was remarkable. Of course, in the fall during rutting season you can smell elk. There is a faint odor in the air if you get close to a herd of elk and the wind's blowing in the right direction. George would ride along a slope next to a hill and he would sniff the air a few times. "My God, there's some elk over there on the other side of that hill," he'd say. "It's breeding season and I believe there's a big old elk over there with a good set of antlers. Let's tie up our horses here and sneak up to the top of the hill and see if we can see them."

They would sneak up to the top of the hill, and, by God, over the hill in a clearing were some female elk with one bull with a beautiful set of antlers that had driven away all the other bulls. There were several things like that that George could do that were almost miraculous.

But I knew how he did it. George knew that the clearing was an excellent place for elk to be and he would go ahead where he could peek at the clearing and see that there were elk there. Then he'd take the people around through the timber, do his sniffing thing, and take them up to the top of the hill and there was this big bull elk. That was impressive. That guy was some hunter and was tipped liberally.

***

I only ran the hunting camp for a short time because I found it interfered with my guiding. I sold the ranch back to a man who had helped finance me so he could build some buildings on it. I didn't want to have anything to do with it. By that time Bob Carmichael was meeting many people through fly-casting, guiding, and teaching fly-fishing, as well as through selling equipment. Many of these sportsmen, who had plenty of money to go fly-fishing, also had money to go hunting. After I left the ranch, Bill, a neighbor who had a little place up Ditch Creek Canyon, was hired to take care of the place. In the fall, Carmichael used to bring up some hunters for Bill to guide.

This one fella was an experienced hunter, an antler hunter. He wanted to get a bigger set of antlers than he already had. He had been on safaris in Africa and could name a whole list of animals he'd shot: Cape buffalo, lions, elephants, and so on. Before this particular trip he wanted to site in a new rifle. The way they did this was by shooting at an empty red Hills Bros. coffee can perched on top of a fence post.

The fella wanted to site in his gun for one hundred yards because he thought he was most likely to get a shot at that distance. If it was over one hundred yards he could aim a little higher and if it was under he could aim a little lower. A bullet, when it leaves a rifle, falls sixteen feet per second unless Isaac Newton was hit on the head with a rotten apple. Hunters had to make allowance for that. Now there are sites you can set if you have time, but in those days it was more practical to use your own judgment to determine how much a bullet was going to fall. So actually at one hundred yards a hunter wouldn't aim where the bullet was going to hit, unless he had his sites set for that distance, in which case he was looking at the target but the rifle was aimed a little higher.

This fella shot once and hit the post below where the can was, so he realized he had to raise his sites. Bill replaced the can on the fence post and stepped off to the side. The fella shot again — it's so tragic you don't want to talk about it — but he blew the top of Bill's head off. Bill was wearing a Stetson hat and like many of the guides he had a red handkerchief wrapped around it so people could see him out in the field. That and some sort of red jacket would usually keep people from shooting them.

It was so tragic, but it wasn't anybody's fault. That was the normal procedure for a guide helping a hunter site in his gun. Maybe the fella's eyes were a little bad. I knew later that the hunter, after he got back home, was very liberal in his help to Bill's family.

***

Meeting all these different types of people in the bars or out in the field was a great way to study human nature, since there were some real characters in Jackson's Hole. People who didn't want to adjust to civilization had a chance of going there and making a living. Also there were, we didn't call them remittance men, but they were sort of half-dudes, never completely taken in by the local population, although some of them did work at times. These were people who had what we used to call an ace in the hole. If they needed money, they could get money from home. Some of them were deliberately kept out there to keep them away from home because they were nuisances.

I met one of those half-dudes in a bar once. He was an intelligent man who loved to read. He had some land along the Snake River on the west side between Wilson and what is now Moose. He was a very inventive guy. I visited him at his cabin one day, and he had a fire in the fireplace partially fed by a tree that had been trimmed and had been pushed through a hole in the side of the cabin. As the end of it burned off he would keep pushing it through the hole in the wall into the fireplace. I don't know how he kept from burning down his cabin.

Once I saw him in his buggy with a nice team of horses. He sat on the buggy's seat, impervious to the horses, reading a book. The reins were tied around something and the horses were moving along, grazing in the field in a relaxed way while he read. It was rumored that he was a law student and a great amateur boxer, maybe a champion in the collegiate field. Perhaps one of the blows he suffered made him, in dude language, a little odd.

***

Another type of character that came to Jackson's Hole was the man who came to get away from demon rum. Of course, Jackson's Hole was one of the worst places this type of person could come, as Carmichael often told me. Not only were there some of the best moonshine stills in the West there, but the local saloons and bars were the social places. That's where people met. Even the good nonjack Mormon Mormons, who never took a drink of whiskey in their lives, would go there to meet people and talk business. There weren't any other places to go.

This one fella I met at a bar and became well acquainted with had a serious case of alcoholism. Frankie was in his late twenties and had come out there to sober up and try to change his habit. But the only place he could meet and talk to people was in a bar, and if he was talking to someone who was drinking that person would generally buy him a drink. He would expect the same thing back.

I told Frankie if he really wanted to get away from it he should go out with one of the trappers. I knew a fella from DuBois who I thought might like the company, so I suggested he spend a couple of months with him. Frankie thought it was a great idea, so I arranged it for him.

Trapping doesn't start until late in the fall, because the animals need real cold weather to grow the luscious fur they have during the winter. That winter fur has to be stabilized to have what is called a prime hide, so that after an animal is skinned and the hide dries, the hair won't shed. So Frankie went to the hills late in the fall with the trapper I knew. I thought it might work for him, and it was better than using the money he had perhaps inherited from back East to be popular in the bar by buying more than his share of the drinks.

I forgot all about it until the next year I came back to Jackson's Hole. Of course, I went to the bar to meet all my friends and there was Frankie. I sat down with him, and he bought me a drink and told me his tale of woe.

He was helping the trapper, but when the snow got deep and it got cold he didn't want to go out much anymore. The trapper would take off with his snowshoes early in the morning and come in late at night or perhaps stay out in a wickiup and come back the next day. The trapper had a ritual when he returned to the cabin. He went outside and took down part of an elk he had frozen, put it on top of a stump, and chopped off a thick slice of steak with his ax. Then he fried his elk steak with little or no conversation, perhaps answering a few questions about what he had caught or where he'd been.

After dinner he lay on his bunk and pulled out a book from a cloth sack alongside his bed and started reading. All he read were love stories — that's it. Frankie was getting cabin fever and he figured he'd have to do something. So one day while the trapper was out, he gathered up the bag with all the love stories in it and took it outside and hid them. This was certainly going to bring conversation. He would wonder where his love stories went, and they would discuss it for a while. Frankie knew he'd have to bring one or two back.

The trapper came in that night, took his ax, chopped off his elk steak, fried it, and they had dinner. Then he went over to his bunk, lay down, and reached for his love stories. They weren't there. But he went to sleep and didn't say a word. The next morning he packed up to go out trapping. Frankie noticed he was taking some extra food and it didn't quite look like what he took out normally to tend his trapline, but he didn't think anything of it.

That night the trapper didn't come back, and Frankie was a little worried. The next night he didn't come back, and Frankie was real worried, and the next night he came in. But he didn't have any martin with him; he just had a pack he put over by his bunk. After supper he went and lay down on his bunk, reached in his pack, and pulled out a love-story book.

"That sonofabitch had been all the way to DuBois and back," Frankie said, "to get some more literature! I couldn't take it anymore. I just couldn't take it anymore. The next sunny day, I didn't know whether I'd get out alive, but I gathered up my junk and put it in a pack and put on my snowshoes and I came out!"

Whether that was an entirely true story or whether it was made up to give him an excuse to get back to the bars, I'm not sure.

CHAPTER NINE

DEMON RUM

"Prohibition never came to Jackson's Hole."
— *Paul Petzoldt*

In the fall of 1927, when I left the Lucas ranch and headed back to school in Idaho, I planned on returning to Jackson the next summer. But it didn't work out that way. The café in Twin Falls where I had been working had been purchased by a businessman from Ohio. When he got a chance to sell the place and return to Toledo to take over another restaurant there, he invited me along and offered me a job. When he assured me I would be able to finish high school in Ohio, I packed my bags.

I became a good waiter while working at several cafés in Toledo, even ones where I had to wear a tux. It was also that summer that I was bitten by the golf bug. I had dreams of becoming a champion golfer as well as a champion mountaineer. I managed to make a little money and finish high school at Scott High in Toledo, which made me eligible to begin college at the University of Idaho.

I was not to see Jackson's Hole again until the spring of 1930. In that time, most of it spent in Toledo, I became more worldly. Toledo was a gangster's paradise. No single gang was dominant in the city. The Capone Gang of Chicago, the Purple Gang of Detroit, and the other gangs around the country had declared Toledo a neutral city, where they could meet and talk things over without shooting each other.

It was also a free port to get liquor in from Canada. Bootlegging was such a good business that it was rumored that the sheriff of the county had spent a great deal of money to get elected, because he was sure to become rich after his first term.

While working at a Chinese restaurant called King Hong Lo, I came into direct contact with many visiting gangsters.

***

Only once did I get personally involved in bootlegging, and it was by accident. I did it sort of as a joke, but it wasn't a joke at all. There was a guy who handled one of the gambling places in Jackson who didn't like me much. We had had a close encounter once. One fall, after the climbing season was over, I went to work for a trucker who operated a small trucking outfit from Salt Lake to Jackson. I would go down to the wholesale places in Salt Lake, sometimes with some cargo but generally with an empty truck, and fill up with orders for the various stores in Jackson.

I had this one order of special packages that were supposed to be presents or something. I didn't quite know what they were, but they were camouflaged like groceries. I had delivered these types of orders a couple of times before, and I noticed that wine and liquor that wasn't bootleg whiskey was appearing in the saloon where this order was being delivered. One time it was a fairly large order, and I thought, "I'm hauling liquor and if I'm stopped it will be my butt, because no one else will know anything about it, of course."

So I opened up one of the packages, and it was wine. My brother, Curly, was visiting at the time. So he made this trip with me and on the way back, when we got into Wyoming, he said, "You're a damn fool for hauling this stuff. Why take these chances? Hauling this stuff across state lines, that's a federal offense."

Whether it was or not I didn't know, but it scared the hell out of me. We got up near Kemmerer, Wyoming, and passed over a fairly large galvanized culvert that went under the highway. "Let's just put this stuff in there and hide it and see what happens," Curly said.

"What will we tell him happened to the stuff?" I asked.

"You tell him we were hijacked," Curly said. "Tell him somebody must have known about the shipment, because the moment we got into Wyoming down there around Kemmerer somebody stopped us on the road. They had a shotgun and they seemed to know what they were looking for and they just unloaded all that stuff you ordered and took it in a car and drove off."

That was my story, and when I told it to Joe, the owner of the saloon, I added, "They also told us it would be dangerous to report it to anybody, so I'm taking a chance telling you about it."

Well, he went back in the kitchen sputtering in Italian and came back out with a butcher knife, but luckily some of the people around were sober enough to grab him.

Later on I wandered into his place one night when he wasn't there. I seldom went into his place, but I didn't see him around so I walked in with a friend. We went over to the roulette wheel, which had something called a gaff. Certain numbers were magnetized and certain balls had some steel in them that could be drawn into this magnet. It wouldn't do it every time but it would do it enough to make a terrific difference in the house's percentage of winning.

If everybody was betting big on other numbers and they weren't betting on the magnetized number, the house could turn on the electricity. Then there was a one in five or one in ten chance that the ball would go into this magnetized slot. Otherwise the chances were one in thirty-eight. There were thirty-six numbers, I believe, and two other slots for zero and double zero, which was the house's advantage on straight odds. If the ball went in the number that was bet on, the winnings were thirty-six to one but actually the odds were thirty-eight to one.

That night I was feeling rather adventurous, a little mischievous. And I noticed there was a lot of betting and this number I thought was a gaff number was open. I had three silver dollars and I put them on that number. The ball came around slower and slower and when it came to that number, zoom, it went right in that hole. Well, these guys knew me and they paid me off, but the way they looked at me, I took the money and left real quick. I never gambled in there again.

The next day, I had coffee with one of the guys who paid me off. He was sort of humorous about it. It wasn't his money; he just worked there. "Who wised you up about our wheel?" he asked. "We had to change the number."

"What do you mean wised me up?" I asked.

"You knew that number was hot," he said.

"What do you mean?" I asked. "You mean you got a crooked wheel in there?"

"No," he said. "I guess you were just lucky."

***

I had met a doctor and his wife who liked spending time in Jackson's Hole. When one of the saloons went up for sale he bought it. But the people of Jackson thought that he shouldn't own it for some reason. I did hear rumors that some people thought he was a "dope fiend." Even though he had money he was a persona non grata in the town of Jackson.

They had assured him that the city council was not going to give him a liquor license, and if he didn't get a license, what the hell was he going to do with a saloon? So he offered it to me for a fraction of what it was worth if I paid him in cash, which I did. So I owned a saloon right off the square in Jackson.

It was the spring before climbing season, so I started operating the saloon. I hired one of the best bartenders I had ever known. He was somewhat of an alcoholic and also a little dishonest. He told me if he needed any money that he never took more than five dollars out of the cash register. Every night he would generally take a small bottle of whiskey off the shelf and take it home, whether I was looking or not.

That bar suddenly became a popular bar in town. So popular that I made it too popular. I was too much competition to the other bars. I made it a rule that anybody working there always greeted the customers by their first names, and if they looked like people who would spend some money — if they had just come in from the cold or from out of town or something — my workers were to buy them their first drink. If the customers bought another drink, which they always did, we were ahead, and if they bought someone else a drink, we were further ahead.

It was customary then, if you bought someone a drink and some change came back, you would leave it on the bar. If you bought another drink, the bartender just collected from what was on the bar. The bartender was named Harris, and one crowded

Saturday night we had to sit down and have a talk. I was watching how he was collecting the money, and it was all going in the till. "We've got to have some moral standards here," I said. "From now on, you cannot collect for the same drink more than three times."

That was the whole spirit of running a saloon and gambling — you had to take advantage of the producers when they were producing. It wasn't a place for a person with ethical standards. It was something I fast knew I couldn't manage and still climb mountains. Before long one of the gamblers came in dealing twenty-one. I knew he was a crossroader. He was handy enough with the cards that he could let people win or let them not win. He would get them into the game but eventually he was going to get their money.

I was supposed to get at least 50 percent of his winnings, but I knew he wasn't giving me my share. I was just another producer to him, as people in the gambling business called people who lost their money — just another sucker.

Since I was doing good business and perhaps was a threat to the other saloons, through the grapevine I heard the city council wasn't going to give me a license either. Of course, this was the time of the real Depression. No one knew at that time how much a liquor license was going to be worth. They became limited by the laws of the state of Wyoming. The number of liquor licenses in a town was determined by the population.

Somebody who had worked at the bar before, and I believe was on the city council, said he would pay me what I had paid for the bar to get out. So I got out.

CHAPTER TEN

BRING 'EM
BACK ALIVE

"Mountain humor oftentimes comes from people who suffer and have a helluva hard time and still come back alive."
— *Paul Petzoldt*

On some occasions, if tourists did not want to climb a mountain but wanted to spend an extra day in the Tetons, I would take them to some nearby waterfalls. To get there we crossed Jenny Lake in a boat that was an official park concession or hiked along the partially built horse trail to Cascade Creek, which runs around the Grand Teton and drops into Jenny Lake. The roar of the beautiful high falls echoed from the surrounding cliffs. This eventually became the site of my climbing school.

It was great to take people there and teach them how to handle the rope, how to belay, and how to locate secure handholds and footholds. I also taught them the voice signals I had developed for belaying, so people could understand each other on the mountain. The roar of the falls was a perfect simulation of the sound of high winds on the top of the Grand Teton.

After the falls, we would climb some fairly interesting cliffs nearby. I went up first and belayed my clients as they followed. It was a frightening experience climbing alongside a waterfall that shot over the cliff to a pool of water gouged out by the falls one hundred feet below. The movement of this water was enough to unnerve anyone, and it gave people practice in climbing under stress. It was a great experiment. People loved it and talked about it to other campers. Others wrote me letters about the waterfall climbs, calling them the highlight of their trips through Yellowstone and Teton parks that year.

Paul (left), twenty three, with Mr. and Mrs. Fred Wittenberger from Ohio, and Glenn Exum. Taken July 14, 1931, at Lupine Meadows, the day before the discovery of the Exum Ridge. (Glenn Exum Collection)

I had one guy come over to the climbing school one day and do quite well in learning the signals and belays and other skills we taught. But as soon as we started up the cliff he grabbed ahold of a tree and started trembling. I thought he might be having a heart attack or stroke or something like that, so I sent the rest of the group up with another instructor and I went back to him. We backed down ten feet or so where we could sit on a log and talk.

He told me he had acrophobia and couldn't control it. He thought doing some climbing would help him get over it. He was a scientist from Cal Tech, where they did a lot of work on the atomic bomb and there are a lot of theoretical scientists. He told me many of his friends there climbed mountains and he wanted to be able to go with them, but he had to get over his fear of heights first and learn something about climbing.

"I don't know about it," I said, "but this is no place for you today. I don't have anything to do for the next couple of days. If you want to, I'll take you out alone and we'll see what we can do."

Many mountain climbers are people who deal with things they can't see or feel. Many are doctors or scientists who normally are dealing with theories — mental stuff, not things done by hand or things you can actually see being done, like building or the moving of materials. Consequently they feel the need to do something physical and to do something they can start and finish in a short time and bring to a successful conclusion.

That is my theory of why so many of these people who were not otherwise into physical endeavor or jobs that took a lot of physical energy were climbing mountains. And of course the English aristocracy didn't shovel shit; they had servants to do that.

The next day he and I came back across the lake and up the trail to where there was a flat space that dropped off over a cliff. I put the scientist on a rope so he could feel he was secure, and we went out onto the flat area where I took ahold of him and pushed him a bit here and there, now and then. He walked at the end of the rope in a little circle on the rock, getting closer and closer to the edge.

By noon, we sat out there and had lunch, and by evening he could sit out on the end of the rope and look over the ledge. The next day we did it again. After that he came back to the climbing school and with a little trembling from time to time went through the whole school. Then I put him with one of our real good guides and he went up the Owen Route and back down again. I'm not sure this sort of treatment would work with all people with acrophobia, but it worked for him.

We wanted people to be frightened; we wouldn't have taken them unless we knew that they'd be frightened. But we wanted them to be frightened in a reasonable way. We didn't want them frightened in a hysterical way so they lost control of their reason and their senses, because then they were dangerous.

There are different kinds of fear. There's fear that you know about and you can handle, which is a normal fear of heights. But there's fear where you get so frightened that you become frantic and have accidents that you wouldn't ordinarily have if you were using your reason.

***

The miscommunication that had caused all the confusion when Glenn discovered the Exum Ridge occurred on many of my climbs. If the rope went around the corner or if the wind was howling, it was difficult to make out what people were saying. This sort of muffled speech was easily misunderstood, as Glenn had misunderstood me.

To combat this, we had developed a set of signals using short distinct words and nothing else. I had started to develop these signals when I was seventeen or eighteen. *On belay, up rope, slack*, and *climbing* are examples of signals we used. Not only were they simple to understand, but they could be distinguished by the number of syllables. This made them more readily interpreted even if they weren't clearly audible in the wind.

When someone was ready to have his partner climb he would yell "on belay!" If the climber was ready, he would respond "climbing!" The belayer would acknowledge this with the fail-safe signal "climb!" and the climb would proceed. Three different signals with three different syllables. Once a person had commenced climbing, if he wanted to drop down and pick a better line, he would yell "slack!" and the person taking in the rope would let some back out. When the climber was ready to go again, he would yell "up rope!" if there was too much slack in the rope, or "climbing!" to begin climbing again, and the belayer would start taking in rope again.

Later, while climbing in Switzerland, I was surprised to learn that the climbing fraternity in Europe had not invented any efficient way to communicate on a mountain. I often think when I see a new invention: Why didn't I think of that damn simple thing? When I joined the ski troops in World War II, I was put in charge of working out the standard operating procedure for mountain evacuations. We used those signals then; that's when they got introduced to the army. It wasn't long before these signals or slight variations of them were being used all over the United States and in England. They are still used throughout most of the world today.

***

In the early thirties the demand for guiding in the mountains increased far beyond my expectations. After the establishment of the park in 1929, people in Yellowstone were encouraging visitors to go down and see their new park near Jackson's Hole. I soon discovered that a business could be built on tourist trade, on people who had never climbed mountains before or had no intention of climbing mountains before they talked to me. This brought a different type of person to the Tetons.

It was a joy climbing with these new mountaineers. They were easy to direct and did not waste time pretending they knew everything and questioning our judgment. To me, guiding was not work but an enjoyable pastime. By setting a slow pace and not exhausting our clients, conversation could take place and people were at ease. They enjoyed the outdoors and the flora and fauna of the mountains.

The climbing school soon proved to be a necessary and efficient part of our guiding. We were able to select climbs more easily. For some clients we suggested conditioning trips up to

Solitude Lake, and by the time they got back they were ready to go on to Yellowstone.

It was a good system. In the school, we could see people in action, and in that kind of action we saw the real person. When you get on a cliff and start climbing with rope and start using the signals and people have to depend on one another, you can actually see what type of person you have. You can see his or her character. In a few minutes you can learn more about people than you might from days of social conversation and social gatherings.

You could see people's reactions when they were belaying somebody else. You could see people's reactions when they went down on a rappel. For instance, one of the things people did is drop the rope that went around their body, which was normally held by their brake hand. By tightening up just a little on that rope they could stop themselves. But sometimes when they got really frightened they would drop that rope, which left them loose to fall, and then they would grab the rope in front of them with both hands, which would make it impossible for them to get back into what we were using then, a Swiss body-belay. They would just have to be lowered with the rope, and we would try to keep them from burning their hands on the rope.

The school was sort of like a thrashing machine; we separated the wheat from the chaff.

***

In Grand Teton National Park's early days, there were no regulations as far as climbing was concerned. Anybody could climb any place they wanted. There was no signing in and no signing out. Of course, the local rangers would have been happy if there were no climbers. They were content to regulate the campgrounds and to build trails. They didn't want to chase foolhardy tourists up above timberline, and I didn't blame them.

Back then, the rangers had the mentality of the cowboys. If they had somewhere to go, they'd walk a half mile to get their horse and would saddle it to ride a quarter mile to the neighbors.

Climbing parties, especially from the various eastern alpine clubs, were descending upon the Tetons, and it was obvious that their techniques were not compatible with the terrain. Eventually, I knew there would be accidents and more deaths on the mountains.

We wondered what would happen in the case of such emergencies. Would we be called on to perform the rescues or to bring down the bodies? The county sheriff did not have the training or desire to do such a job. We weren't really sure if it was the sheriff's duty anyway, or that of the park rangers. It wasn't clear who had the authority of enforcing the law in Teton National Park.

One evening, Phil Smith and I had just finished our supper and were sitting around the campfire near my tent in the Jenny Lake campground. I was anticipating an early retirement in a cozy bed, since I had just returned from a climb on the Grand Teton that day. We heard some excited conversation going on in another camp, so we moseyed over to investigate the commotion.

A very excited woman was demanding that the park ranger go look for her husband immediately. His dinner had been ready for over half an hour, and he was never late for dinner. Certainly something dreadful must have happened to him and their son, she said. The two of them had left early that morning to hike to the other side of Jenny Lake. They had promised they would return for supper.

The ranger was being tactful and explaining to her that it was just starting to get dark and that she shouldn't worry. They had taken the boat across the lake that morning, and the ranger had already learned that they hadn't reserved a boat for the evening. He expected they would be walking down the trail to the campground from near Hidden Falls, and since there was going to be moonlight that night, they would probably find their way in later. This did not satisfy the woman.

Her husband, a professor from a well-known eastern university, was very punctual, and if he had not arrived she knew that something was definitely wrong. The rangers persuaded her to wait a little while. We returned to my campground, but the silence did not last long. As darkness started to set in, the woman became hysterical. She drove down to the nearest telephone at Mr. Gabbey's store and tried to call her congressman. She wanted the authorities from Washington, D.C., to order the rangers to go look for her husband and son, who must be lying out there injured or bleeding to death and certainly would not survive the night.

More rangers arrived as the woman's hysteria and demands increased. Her attempts to reach her congressman or the president of the United States were impressing park officials. They were also impressing Phil and me, who were listening to all of this. Obviously, no one was going to sleep in the campground that night unless someone found her husband. I felt sorry for the rangers. It was silly to go out and look for the pair in the middle of the night, especially since the woman didn't know where they had gone.

We did know they had crossed the lake in the boat. The boatman thought they probably went up toward Symmetry Spire and Mount St. John. In order to quiet the campground and help out the rangers, who had no training for a rescue and were not enthusiastic about nosing around the peaks even during the day, Phil and I took off in pursuit. The rangers arranged for a small motorboat to take us across the lake in the dark, and we headed up the steep slope toward Symmetry Spire.

As often as I could, I halted for a catnap. But Phil, having no one to joke or laugh with, would wake me up and we would continue looking. We started to yoo-hoo to see if anyone would answer. There were only our own echoes from the cliffs that broke the stillness of the night. After we were almost hoarse from yoo-hooing, the sun came up and we saw footprints. Phil still had his great sense of humor and said we were about yoo-hooed out, and maybe we should go back. But we followed the footprints up the snow to where they disappeared onto some boulders and grassy parts of the mountain.

We now could see over much of the valley between the small peaks, and we could also view the sides of the mountains. Phil was not sure about his yoo-hoo, but he was sure that anyone still alive could hear mine. Finally, we had cleared our consciences and convinced ourselves we had done everything we could. We made our way back down to the boat landing where, fortunately, the boatman had just dropped off some tourists. He gave us a quick bounce back to the campground.

We went to report to the woman and the rangers exactly where we had been and what we had done, and also to find out what the situation was. I was astonished to see that only an empty campsite was left where the woman had been the night before. The tent was gone, the fire was out, and there was no car parked there. There was nothing.

We found the ranger, and he told us that when he had gotten up in the morning and went to see how the woman, who had calmed down after we left, had made it through the night, the family was gone. Even Phil found it hard to laugh about the situation, although later we told many jokes about it. While we were up there yoo-hooing, the husband and son had returned and, finding out all the commotion his wife had caused, the husband had packed up his family and fled in the night without notifying the rangers.

We compared him to an Arab who packed his tent under cover of darkness and fled to avoid his enemies. Of course, they were never heard from again. I think the park service was so relieved to have the situation resolved that they didn't pursue him to get more information about his strange adventure.

***

We found out real quick that people didn't like to be rescued. Lost kids would often hide from rescuers because they were afraid they were in trouble with their parents. Adults reacted in a different way. Their egos were affected because they had made a mistake and had to be saved. Macho types never wanted to be rescued, or they probably did want to be rescued but they didn't want to admit they made a mistake or had any faults or errors in judgment.

One case like this was when a fella from Sierra Club fell on Mount Owen. We were still using the strap-iron pitons made by the blacksmith in Jackson then, and for rappeling we would put a short length of rope through the hole at the end of the piton and tie it in a loop. Then we'd put the rappel rope through that loop. I had a couple of these on Mount Owen and after I had rappeled down last I left the piton with the rope in it.

The next summer a group from the Sierra Club came and they had a crack climber who led part of the group up Mount

Owen. On the way down he belayed the rest of the group and then was going to rappel down using the piton and rope I had left there the year before. The rope had been there over the winter and perhaps was a little rotten and it failed him. He took quite a fall and was pretty well cut up and had suffered some sprains and other injuries.

My guides went up to help bring him down. There were others there, but my guides were the ones who really brought him down. Of course, he was rushed right to the hospital. Afterwards, we learned that he was a rich young man. He was one of those types that had really made a success early in life. He had inherited several million dollars by the time he was twenty-one, a real success story. We thought, well, we had almost saved this guy's life and we started to imagine that when he got out of the hospital he would come to thank us and dish out one-hundred-dollar bills like he was dealing cards. Instead, we learned more about human nature and how people react after they're rescued. They don't want to face anyone, especially their rescuers. He headed back to California and never sent us even a thank-you note.

I guess people expected that the park paid for the rescues, but the park had no money. I never got paid for helping the park. Later on, I got no pay for going up Devil's Tower and rescuing stranded parachutist George Hopkins, although the park drove me up there and paid for my food. Even with the plane rescue on Mount Moran in 1950, the park finally said it could authorize paying me ten dollars a day.

***

I returned to Jackson's Hole in 1931 a different type of mountaineer. I was twenty-three. I had gained a national reputation and had been granted the concession, giving me exclusive guiding rights to the area within Grand Teton National Park. That gave me more prestige among the locals too. I was happy about the whole situation.

With increased prestige came increased responsibility. I quickly realized I would have to train more guides to keep up with business demands. Even though Gibb Scott had not continued his guiding career, others had started to move in on the fringes. Climbing clubs would often have their own guides to take people to the top of some of the nearby minor peaks, or out on the glacier.

It took a long time before the park had any enthusiasm whatsoever for climbing. The park service was friendly and tolerant but not enthusiastic about what I was doing. So I was surprised when I was asked to come down to see the park superintendent, Charles Smith, who was new. The superintendents seem to come through the system quite fast. Perhaps one of the reasons for this was that, like the forest service, the park service didn't want park superintendents to become so well acquainted with the locals that they were their friends and might make decisions based on that friendship. Promotions usually meant transfers too, so that no jealousy and competition would arise.

Generally, if there was anything to be said to me by the park it was done through the chief ranger or one of the ordinary employees. I thought I might be in trouble, so I went there somewhat apprehensive. When he got me in the office the first question the superintendent asked was, "Do you think I can climb the Grand Teton?"

I said sure. No superintendent had ever climbed it and except for Phil Smith and Fryxell I didn't think anybody from the park had climbed the Grand. "I want to climb it," he said.

"Fine," I said. "I'll take you myself."

Then he told his secretary to have his chief ranger, whose name was Hanks, come in. I don't think he knew I was there, and when he saw me he looked puzzled. "I want to climb the Grand Teton," the superintendent said. "What do you think about it?"

Hanks made some noncommittal remark that was entirely neutral, so the superintendent went on. "I've talked this over with Petzoldt, and he said he'll personally take us up." When the superintendent said "us" I saw Hanks flinch a little. "Of course I want you to come along, so go out and check our schedules and let's give Petzoldt a date when we can start," the superintendent said.

I could see Hanks wasn't pleased. Maybe he didn't want to be associated with the group of people who climbed mountains.

There was a definite cleavage between the people who rode horses and the people who climbed mountains. There wasn't much meeting of the minds between these two types.

A date was set and off we went. I decided to take them on the Exum Ridge, which wasn't too difficult for them. It went well, except while we were up on the ridge a small storm came over. The clouds were close over our heads. There was some static electricity, which I had learned not to fear really, but it always made me anxious. I could always tell when we had static electricity because my eyebrows would start tingling. Other times we'd hear the ends of our ice axes buzzing.

That day I got quite a bite from it. I was climbing up a different way to avoid what we called the Friction Pitch. I was going up a chimney that involved a little harder climbing, but one from which I would have a firm belay. It was quite exciting for them but absolutely safe. As I got up there spread-eagle in the chimney, my eyebrows were really tingling. I reached out my hand to put it on the other wall and I saw some sparks fly from my hand to the rock. I got a real bite all the way up my arm to my shoulder. Even the next day I could feel in my shoulder where evidently my muscle had tensed up from the shock.

We got up to the top with no problems and on the descent we did some rappeling, which was exciting for them as it was for most people who weren't hardened mountaineers. It was the way we had learned to avoid the Crawl on the way down — by rappeling down Owen's unclimbable wall. From the top of this cliff you can't see the bottom because of the overhang, and once you get about halfway down your feet can't touch wall and you're just hanging out there in the air. It's a lot of height and it's on the southwest side. Generally there's a wind rushing up from the Lower Saddle; it is squeezed through the channels between the mountains so it really moves. It's an exhilarating rappel.

I used to do a little act and I taught my guides to do it too. If the people were frightened at this spot, I acted as if it was nothing. If people were blasé or a little careless, I acted as if the move was more difficult than it really was; I acted more tense. I tried to reflect the mood of the climb. That way I could make it more enjoyable.

One time I had some people up there and I wanted to get down as quickly as possible. There were some black clouds coming in from over Idaho Falls way. They were black clouds with fat bottoms and I knew when they hit the Tetons we'd have some lightning. The wind was howling. To get our rappel rope to the bottom of the cliff without tangling we had to coil it in a certain way. I got out on the edge and I threw the rope over. It went down about halfway and then blew back up over my head. My clients were very impressed, and even my best acting couldn't relax them.

But the climb with the superintendent and his reluctant ranger was uneventful and enjoyable. I think the superintendent did it out of curiosity or maybe to say he had been the first park superintendent to climb the Grand Teton. I don't think either one of them ever climbed the mountain again, not as far as I know. I think Hanks rather enjoyed seeing how it was done and perhaps, in the end, he thought it gave him another type of status with the people who worked for the park. But if it did that, it probably gave him a lower status with the people who ain't lost nothin' up there.

***

Glenn's first guiding trip in the park was more of an adventure than we had anticipated. I sent him out to climb Mount Teewinot, a mountain visible from Jenny Lake and one that most people thought was the Grand Teton itself. When looking from the campground, the Grand Teton was completely hidden behind it. With its spires, Teewinot would be an impressive mountain if it were there alone without the rest of the Tetons.

Glenn's two clients were enthusiastic men but somewhat uncoordinated. Climbing Teewinot in one day was a long but fairly easy climb if one kept on the right route. They started out early in the morning and made good progress toward the top, which they eventually made. During the climb, on a safe ledge one of the men tried to push the other up over a little pitch and the man on top fell on the other one. That was the closest to a serious injury that they had on the trip, but the climb did take longer than I had expected. The route was a little difficult to follow, and Glenn led the climb in a safe, unhurried manner.

It was dark before they reached the bottom of the mountain. Then they had to go through some trailless country between the base of the mountain and Jenny Lake. Unknown to Glenn, there were some beaver ponds between them and their destination. It was the only way back, however, and the three men waded through the beaver ponds where the water got deeper and deeper and the water plants got thicker and thicker.

They arrived at the campfire at Jenny Lake wet and covered with moss. Everyone around the place had a great laugh at their expense, but the two clients laughed too. It had been the greatest adventure of their lives and they thought they were real mountaineers and explorers. They left the next day, two of the most satisfied customers I ever had in the mountains.

They weren't the only ones who got lost in beaver ponds. A group of people from one of the leading mountaineering clubs in the country came to the Tetons once with great trips planned for their stay at Jenny Lake. They were going to climb these mountains one day and another mountain the next day and another mountain the next day. They showed me their itinerary when they first arrived and I thought, gosh, this is an ambitious itinerary. I was sure they wouldn't make a third of the peaks they planned to climb during their short stay.

Having arrived early in the morning, they set up their tents and had a brief lunch. Their enthusiasm was unlimited and, of course, there was a whole afternoon ahead. Some of the people said they would stay in camp and have supper ready for the others in the evening. The rest were gung ho to take the almost completed trail up to Surprise and Amphitheater lakes, where they could view Mount Owen, the Grand Teton, and Teewinot from a short distance.

The information they got from the rangers was that it was about six miles from Jenny Lake to Amphitheater Lake, traveling back and forth on the switchbacks of the trail. This didn't seem like much. They thought they could walk about three miles per hour and it would take them two or three hours to get to Amphitheater Lake and maybe less time to come down. So they'd be back in time for dinner in the evening, since it didn't get dark until about eight-thirty.

In those days, I was beginning to give trail information by hours, because on the map the mileage traveled didn't take into consideration the altitude gained. I was transforming altitude into miles so flat-country people could understand. But the rangers didn't tell this group six miles and three thousand feet, which in my system translated into an eighteen- to twenty-two-mile hike on level ground without heavy packs. So actually they were starting out on a hike equivalent to about twenty miles. These flat-country people didn't know what they were up against.

We also knew by then that if a person climbed fast, he would be exhausted quickly. You had to pace yourself. Anybody who has been to a track meet understands that. If a person starts out running a mile as someone who is running the one-hundred-yard dash, he ain't going to make more than two or three hundred yards before he faints. Exuberance of newly arriving people who were not used to the altitude resulted in quick exhaustion, a loss of enthusiasm, and quick trips on to Yellowstone.

While talking to one of the participants later I got the details of their strange climb. Mountain humor oftentimes comes from people who suffer and have a helluva hard time and still come back alive. This was one of those humorous occasions.

These people started out fast and before long some got tired and the pace had to be slowed down for them. But they wouldn't give up. When they reached Amphitheater Lake, the shadows of the Tetons were well over toward the Wind Rivers. Not long after they started down, lightning began to hit the tops of the mountains, and a small cloudburst descended upon the valley. Two of the leaders of the drenched group said they would run ahead and tell those waiting that the group would be late for supper, and would make sure there was a hot dinner waiting for them when they did arrive.

The two most experienced people took off through the thunder and lightning and ran down to Jenny Lake as fast as they could. The others continued to follow the new trail until they missed a turnoff. They hadn't noticed, on the way up, that at a hairpin turn where the trail to Amphitheater switched back, another trail continued straight to Bradley Lake. Unknowingly, the group missed the corner and took off to Bradley Lake, leaving the route to Jenny Lake behind.

Finally, the storm eased off a bit and the exhausted climbers found themselves at a lake. They knew they hadn't passed a lake on the way up, and someone figured out that it was Bradley Lake. In the meantime, they could see car headlights out beyond Cottonwood Creek about a mile across the sagebrush flat toward Timbered Island. What to do? Of course, the logical thing to do was to cross country, and once they reached the highway they could go from there to the campground or maybe even catch a ride.

So they headed for the lights on the highway. Soon they were in a big beaver pond or swamp. Luckily the rain stopped about that time and I think there was some moonlight. They finally made it through the swamp covered with what we then called Exum Goo. But then they came to Cottonwood Creek, which is a river to ford safely only with a rope. They had developed great judgment by then and knew they couldn't get across the roaring stream. They walked up a ways and came to a bridge. From there they got out to the highway and back to Jenny Lake at 4 A.M.

Meanwhile, adding to the humor were the actions of the two leaders who had gone ahead. When the rest of the group wasn't down by midnight, they became very worried. Despite the fact that they were tired, the two men took another person and started to run back up the trail to see what had happened. Traveling through the night they made it all the way to Surprise Lake and finally returned in time for a late breakfast.

That drained that group's enthusiasm a bit for climbing. Perhaps later they got back enough energy to make one minor climb in their week's stay. That was the American Alpine Club, but we won't identify them.

CHAPTER ELEVEN

DON'T BUCK
THE ODDS

"Back of the bar in a solo game sat dangerous Dan McGrew, and watching his luck was his light-o'-love, the lady that's known as Lou."
— *Robert Service*

G ambling was never legal. Many times they tried to make gambling legal in Wyoming, but every time it came up at the state legislature — and this I can't prove, but this is what was generally thought — people in Las Vegas would give a couple of preachers in Wyoming a lot of money to get out and go all over the state preaching against it and getting the people aroused. Legalized gambling could never get through the legislature. The people in Las Vegas would do that with practically any state in the West that tried to legalize gambling; they would pour money into the opposition.

Although it was illegal, the authorities rarely cracked down, at least in Jackson. There was one famous case involving a man with power in the town who used to go on periodic drinking binges. Generally he would drink enough to pass out or almost pass out and some kind person would take him home. A stranger came in and bought a saloon — paid a high price for it — and this gentleman was drinking there one night and was pretty much in his cup. The owner of the saloon had a bouncer and he threw the gentleman out, or escorted him out.

The next day a truck backed up to the saloon. Some men went in and pulled out most of the slot machines, threw them in the back of the truck, and on the way to the dump smashed them with axes and threw them out. People said, well, he sure done learnt his lesson.

There was one time when gambling in Jackson was temporarily closed down. A congressman from Wyoming was head of the committee that was investigating the eastern gangs in the United States. At one of the hearings a gangster asked the congressman if he knew what was going on in his home state. The gangster publicly questioned why the congressman, who was heading this investigation, hadn't investigated his own state, because in Jackson's Hole gambling was flourishing. That took overnight to get to the governor of Wyoming and the governor phoned the sheriff of Jackson's Hole. The next day all the slot machines were down in the basements and there was no gambling.

It started up again later, but it was getting rougher and rougher. Some real criminal types were starting to come into Jackson's Hole. Eventually, the Mormon newspaper from Salt Lake started to put out some publicity against Jackson's Hole because of its gambling. I suppose because there were a lot of Mormons in Jackson's Hole and nearby Idaho, and perhaps some of the jack Mormons were coming over there and losing some money.

At *one* time, a reporter was up there and he went into one of the saloons and was taking some pictures of people around the craps table or around the twenty-one table. When this newspaperman went into the men's room one of the gamblers followed him in and took away his camera and film and beat him up a little bit. When that hit the headlines in Salt Lake it was too much. For gambling in Jackson, that was all she wrote.

***

Some of the people who came to Jackson for the season to run the crap games were gambleholics. Some of those guys working there, the ones I knew very well like Varley, might leave in the fall with fifteen or twenty thousand dollars, which was a helluva lot of money then. But the next spring, when the saloon owners wanted to open up the gambling, they generally had to send Varley money for transportation back to Jackson. He'd spend all summer cheating and fleecing the producers in Jackson, and then go down and be a producer himself at one of the big gambling joints at Little Rock or Las Vegas or Cuba or some damn place.

I never made much money gambling in Jackson. The people there were too wise. You had people sitting around in the poker games, housemen or representatives, who could use all sorts of tricks. They could deal seconds and they could cheat like hell. I was too smart to get into that. I did make some money playing other games with the gamblers.

There was one game sort of like shuffleboard. You took a round, heavy disc and shoved it down a long narrow table to get it as close to the edge as you could without it falling off. Then another person would throw one to hit your disc and knock it off. Boy, I was awfully good at that. I seldom had to extend myself. I would always play well enough to generally win. I was sort of a slicker there. I got one of these gamblers hooked one night for about twelve hundred dollars, and he said he'd pay me the next day. You could trust their word that they were going to pay. They never said they were going to pay and then didn't. Gamblers couldn't do that and then stay in the country. The next day he paid me off, but he was right at me again trying to get back his money.

Of course, that's when you got 'em hooked. That's how they hook 'em in Las Vegas. They lose some money and they think, gosh, they've got this amount invested so their luck is bound to change or it should change. That's the way the suckers feel after they stuff the slot machines full of money. They think, gosh, it's gotta have a jackpot now; it's full of money. You know if they think like that, they're real suckers. Or if they think there's such a thing as luck outside of odds. Those are the suckers who keep towns like Las Vegas going.

***

I started playing poker when I was young, because gambling was a pastime in those days and there was always a card game in the pool hall. They played games at the Elks Club and the other clubs around Twin Falls. But I was just in little games and I was losing money. I was working at the Perrine Café in Twin Falls. My boss was what they called in those days an old crossroader, who perhaps at one time made his living by gambling. He told me I shouldn't gamble. But, he said, if I was going to gamble I should learn how to win. Then he taught me how.

The first thing he taught me was just some basic judgment about cards. But then he also taught me the odds. Say a gambler has an ace, two, three, and four. A lot of silly gamblers will make a substantial bet on drawing a five on the last card. Well, theoretically, you only have one chance in thirteen of drawing a five. So what are you going to win if you draw a five? Are you going to win thirteen times what you risk? That's the way you have to think. If you think that way, you'll see that you're silly making that kind of bet.

Then he taught me how to bluff, the odds of bluffing. How many people are still holding cards? It's pretty hard to bluff against two or three people. If it's just one guy, that's when you want to bluff. I'd figure the type of hand I had against the type of hand he had. Is there a 50 percent chance he'd call it? Is it 20 percent? If so, then you'd better bluff, because that's when you win money.

If you have cards that *look* like a cinch, you can bet quite a bit. Bet enough so he isn't going to call, unless he has a decent hand; and then you may have him beat anyway. But you raise the stakes because you figure there's a 50 percent chance he's going to fold up. He's got to be awfully brave to call that money if you've got a possibility of beating him. So if he doesn't call it and you were bluffing, you show it to him. Especially early in the game. Then you sort of laugh in a good-natured way. That's setting him up for the coup de grâce. Later, when you know you have a cinch, but you've antagonized him so much he'll think you don't, he'll shove in a bunch. Then he calls and that's the way you break him. You use that bluffing method to set him up for the kill.

My boss also taught me how to remember cards, and that, he said, isn't cheating. Mainly, though, good poker-playing was having your money on the odds and doing a certain type of acting. Early in the game, when you've got a few hands and you are bluffing, you go through some mannerisms. Later when you have a cinch and you are pushing at the pot, trying to get him to call you, you go through those same mannerisms.

I picked it up pretty quick. I started to win money. Well, I think naturally I was a person of pretty good judgment. I was always thinking about the odds and not to go in just because I felt like I had hope or wanted to win the pot. Don't go in when the odds are not in your favor. If the odds are in your favor, you generally have to be pretty unlucky to lose.

By the time I was nineteen or twenty I was a very smart gambler. I was better than the local yokels, but I wasn't ready to go break Las Vegas.

***

In Jackson, I played cards with a local group of businessmen. We played Cour d'Alene solo, which was a high-rolling and intricate game, maybe even harder to play than bridge. It was a gambling game, evidently popular in the early days, because it appears in Robert Service's poems about the gold rush.

The group I used to play with included Homer Richards, who had sold his place down on Jenny Lake and at that time owned the hotel where John Emery shot Fernie Hubbard in the back; Mike Yokel, onetime world champion wrassler when wrestling was somewhat honest and not entirely fake like it is now; and several others. It was a group of about twenty, and every night there generally was a game. Sometimes those games would last all night, and sometimes, with people coming and going, they might last for a couple of days continuously.

Our games weren't too high-rolling, but if a person was really unlucky or didn't know how to play he could lose forty or fifty dollars in a night, which was quite a bit in those days. There was one fella, everyone knew, who if he got a chance would cheat. So we had to watch him carefully. He was one of the leading citizens of the town. I never made any great amount of money playing solo.

My biggest night winning at the poker table was in Paris during the war or maybe it was at the Ramshorn Ranch up Ditch Creek. I got some hunters there one time, four or five of them. They didn't want to go out to a big camp; they just wanted to ride out in the daytime from the ranch and hunt. They were the first hunters I ever knew who flew in on their own plane. They were playing poker viciously against one another for pretty damn high stakes. I didn't think about joining them until one of the fellas asked me one night if I played poker.

"I sure do," I said. "I'm pretty good at it." So they asked me to join them and I did. The first night I went along, learning them and how they played, and I didn't do much. But then I got real lucky and before they left I had enough to pay off a lot of the mortgage. I think I won close to three thousand dollars. They were happy about it, and it was legitimate poker. I don't think any of them cheated and I certainly didn't. I never learned how to deal cards or how to mark cards like some of the crossroaders did. I just learned how to play poker.

***

At times, movie actors still remembered to this day were invited up to Jackson's Hole on hunting trips in the fall for free. Out in the hunting camps they would have poker games. Each of the gamblers dressed, talked, and acted like another dude hunter and he would be the slicker who fleeced the actors of just a slight amount of their money, which was considerable for big-name actors of the day. There were some big losses by big names in Jackson's Hole.

Bob Carmichael had wealthy clients all over the United States who appeared at certain times every year to take their vacations trout fishing. Some of them also liked to gamble. I had a most exciting experience with one of Bob's fishermen one fall after the climbing season was over. As a matter of fact, this person asked Bob if I was available as a fishing guide, because I had guided him on a short trip once before.

This fella was quite a practical joker and he would try to play jokes on Bob and me and everyone, and he was pretty good at it. He had a business in San Diego, a profitable one, I understood. After our fishing trip, I wanted to go to California to visit some relatives. He had arranged transportation from Jackson to Salt Lake City, where he was going to catch a Western Airlines champagne flight down to Los Angeles. He agreed to take me along as his guest.

The fishing was over, but he stayed in Jackson for a couple of days. On the morning we were going to leave we planned to meet at the Wort Hotel where he was staying. I didn't go with him to Jackson the evening before, but Bob had told me that this particular client liked to put on a bender once in a while. I arrived at the hotel quite early, had breakfast, and sat down at the bar to wait, thinking that if he didn't show soon I would call up to his room.

At the end of the bar three men were talking very audibly and excitedly. The words I heard went something like this, "We've got to get a plane and get Woody down to Salt Lake and catch a plane down to San Diego right away before the sonofabitch gets home, because we've got to get these checks cashed before he stops them. We've been through this before and had checks stopped on us before and we can't do anything about it."

I knew what happened lots of times to dudes who drank a little. A druggist in town had concoctions that could be added to almost any drink that made people sleepy. They would go to bed, since they had lost all their money, or if they had a lot of money to spend, it would make them feel they were winning when they were losing and would produce all sorts of other moods. Also, the gamblers were good at setting the tone for these sort of things, so people often woke up in the morning with larger losses than they expected.

I was suspicious, since they had mentioned San Diego, that my friend was the victim. I had heard the figure four thousand dollars. I thought, "Boy, if it's him, he's really been taken for a ride." I left the bar and went to his room. After a few knocks he came to the door and let me in. It was obvious he'd been on one of Bob Carmichael's benders. "Are you still able to go to Salt Lake today?" I asked.

"Sure," he said. "I'll get dressed and we'll have some coffee and I'll be all right."

"What did you do last night?" I asked.

"I did a little gambling," he said. "But the last part of the night's a little hazy. I don't remember too much about it."

"You got any money left?" I asked.

He looked in his pocketbook and said, "Yeah, I got about twelve dollars left."

"How much did you have in there yesterday?" I asked.

"I generally carry about four hundred dollars," he said.

"Did you write any checks?" I asked.

"I don't know," he said. "I'll find out." When he looked in his checkbook he nodded, "Yeah, there's four checks missing."

"How much were they for?" I asked. He didn't know. "Downstairs at the end of the bar I heard one figure of four thousand dollars."

"Oh my God," he said. "I guess there's enough in the bank to cover it."

"Do you want to cover it?" I asked.

"I don't know," he said. "Maybe somebody took advantage of me. I don't remember."

When I found out it was a joint account with his wife I told him what to do. "Don't you dare call out from this hotel. If you do, every word that you say will be heard by somebody else. Get dressed and we'll go down and have some coffee, and then we'll sneak around to the telephone company and you call your wife."

"What are you planning on doing?" he asked.

"I'm planning on your wife going in there today and withdrawing all the money from that account and putting it in another, so when those checks get there, there won't be any money to pay for them."

He asked me if that was a crime, and I said it wasn't, considering the circumstances. And besides, there's no way they could make him pay, because gambling was illegal and it's not illegal to stop checks. So that's what we did.

Perhaps this is the first time I've ever told that story, because I never could have told it in Jackson's Hole. I think that would have been a little dangerous with some of the gambling characters who frequented the country at that time. But that wasn't the end it.

When we arrived at Salt Lake early the next day my friend still had a hangover. I don't know if it was from his night of superdrinking at the hotel or if he had indeed been drugged. Since I was acquainted with Salt Lake I knew of an Italian spaghetti place that sold wine, which may have been allowed in restaurants at that time. However, when we got to the restaurant it no longer served wine. Prohibition had come and was being carefully enforced in the good Mormon state of Utah. As I've often said, prohibition never came to Jackson's Hole. The revenuers didn't want to come over the pass. It was a lot of trouble, and they, maybe unrealistically, thought that it would be the last pass they ever made.

So my friend still hadn't had a drink when we got on the Western Airlines plane to Los Angeles, which was advertised as the champagne flight, because when it got in the air they served champagne. Planes in those days had tables that folded down from the wall and the seats were on both sides of the table. The flight wasn't crowded, so my friend sat in one seat and I sat across the aisle in another because I wanted to look out that side of the plane as we flew out of Utah.

There was one stewardess attending, and no sooner had we gotten in the air than my friend called her over and started sweet-talking her. She put down the table, left, and returned with a full bottle of champagne and a glass. When she walked back toward the front of the plane I followed her. Since my friend had played a couple of jokes on me I thought this was a good time to play one on him.

"By what authority are you serving alcohol in the sovereign state of Utah?" I asked the stewardess.

"We're in the air," she said.

"I'm a bishop in the church," I said. I didn't say what church, but there's only one church to be a bishop of in Utah and there are a lot of bishops. Maybe that was a bad thing to do. I continued, "I want you to go to the pilot immediately and I want you to ask him by what authority he permits the serving of alcohol in the sovereign state of Utah."

She ran in there, and I think my friend had part of a glass of wine consumed by that time. But she came out and rushed directly to his table and picked up his half-full glass and the bottle and brought it back up to the front of the plane. She explained to him that while they were sure it was all right over other states, they didn't know whether they were serving alcohol illegally over Utah.

He didn't get his champagne back until we got over Las Vegas. I didn't tell him until a year later that I had pulled this joke on him. He took it very well.

***

One of the ways of hiding money was through the slot machines. In those days they had dollar slot machines that would take silver dollars. Those dollars could be kept anywhere. They wouldn't rot; they were eternal and untraceable and perhaps wouldn't have to be reported in a saloon's earnings.

One night I saw a wonderful thing happen that made one slot machine player very angry. The reason slot machines are so vicious is because a lot of people mistakenly think that if you put a lot of money in them that they're ready for the jackpot. A fella had been playing this dollar machine for some time and had a lot of investment in it. He went back to the bar with a bill to get more silver dollars.

In Jackson at that time we had a very likeable young man who unfortunately had the moniker of Dummy. He was deaf and dumb. But Dummy made a pretty good living by going from saloon to saloon to anywhere there were slot machines and just pulling the handles. Lots of times when people are putting money into the machine they're one silver dollar ahead, so when they press the lever they think it's their last dollar. But there is still one in the machine. The same goes for the fifty-cent and the quarter and the nickel ones; there were slot machines all the way down the line that somebody might have left an extra piece of silver in.

Just as the fella turned and went to the bar here comes Dummy and he pulls the lever. He hit the jackpot! Dollars came out and rolled all over the floor. There was also a special thing that if a person hit the jackpot he got an extra hundred or two from the bar. The fella getting change sputtered, but public opinion wasn't on his side. Everybody cheered when Dummy hit the jackpot.

CHAPTER TWELVE

THE LEGEND
OF JOHN EMERY

"Candy is dandy but liquor is quicker."
— *Ogden Nash*

Through the years, as I was attempting to build up a profitable guiding business with thoughts of owning some land in Jackson's Hole, life went on. There were parties, there was romance, fights among the cowboys, rodeos. Often, Glenn Exum and I were invited to various ranches for dinner, not because we were handsome young westerners but because the dude girls needed escorts, and sometimes even the dude women.

I remember one time we were invited to spend a weekend at a ranch to supervise it and entertain two dude women. The owners of the ranch were away and didn't want their guests to arrive and find nobody there. Both women probably exceeded us in age by ten years. As we soon found out, they were not only coming out to Jackson's Hole to view the Tetons, but they also expected some romantic action with some local cowboys. Though Glenn and I weren't bronc riders, we were accepted in their absence.

The weekend was an enjoyable one for me, and although my learning was not connected with mountain climbing, it was very worthwhile. I don't know how Glenn fared, but he had by far the better-looking one of the two. In all the years since, he has never mentioned the lost weekend. Maybe he wants to forget it, but it lingers in my fond memories.

Such romantic adventures culminated in one of the most memorable nights of my history in Jackson's Hole. It was a closer brush with death than many I had had on the mountain.

Of course, Glenn was involved. He had a date with Dorothy Redmond, a beautiful young dude gal whose father owned the Red Rock Ranch along the Gros Ventre River. Dorothy had a friend visiting, so Glenn needed a stand-in and I was a very willing victim.

As we did almost every Saturday night, we went to the Jenny Lake dance hall, where Glenn would also be playing in the orchestra. He wielded an effective saxophone that night, but every once in a while he would get a break to dance with Dorothy. Her friend and I danced a few dances and then partook in another Saturday-night ritual. We went out to a Buick parked in the shadows just out of the light of the dance hall, where we traded a dollar for a small bottle of local moonshine. The whiskey came from a still up Cash Creek, considered by many as one of the best around. The liquor was clean, free of fusel oil or anything else that could blind or paralyze the drinker for up to a week.

With our bottle in hand, we walked down to the rippling waters of Cottonwood Creek and sat down on a log. After a couple drinks we engaged in some innocent romance that in those days was called necking. When we emerged back into the dance hall something terrific had happened.

People were gathered around Dorothy, who was crying and had a bloody nose. The deputy sheriff was ordering Glenn and the orchestra to get back onstage and to start playing to try and calm the nervous crowd. Most of the people were sitting or standing at the sides of the dance hall in silence, except for one fella who was strutting around in the middle of the dance floor.

It was a mystery to me, so I asked some of the people with Dorothy what had happened. They told me she had been dancing with Glenn and this fella asked to cut in, but she refused. So he gave her a haymaker in the nose. Then they pointed to John Emery, the guy I had seen strutting around on the dance floor. "Is anybody going to do anything about it?" I asked.

"No, that's John Emery!" someone said.

I don't know to this day what prompted me to do what I did next. Maybe it was the hooch. Next thing I knew I was in John Emery's face asking him if he was the one who hit Dorothy

Redmond. "You don't want to make anything out of it, do you?" he asked.

"Yes, you sonofabitch. Come on outside," I said. When we reached the porch and squared off, he swung at me with a haymaker that I managed to duck. I came back between his arms with a slight blow to the Adam's apple and another blow low enough that would have barred me from a regular fight. He staggered, and I took advantage of it by putting my shoulder to him and knocking him backwards over the porch banister onto the gravel several feet below.

By the time he got to his feet, I was down with him to continue the fight. But he bent over in a way that I couldn't hit him so I stood there waiting for him to straighten up. I did have some boxing experience. Gene Tunney's former sparring partner was a cook at the Perrine Café in Idaho where I worked one winter, and he had trained me well. He had also convinced me to save all my money and put it on Tunney when he fought Jack Dempsey for the heavyweight title, September 23, 1926. I got ten-to-one odds on that fight and won several hundred dollars, which was more money than I had ever seen. Years later, Tunney and I would almost come to blows on Betty Woolsey's lawn over an argument about Chinese politics, but that's another story.

At that moment, I wasn't thinking about any boxing lessons I had received. People had streamed out of the dance hall by then and luckily had pulled me away and grabbed John Emery and straightened him up. When they did, someone was wise enough to take the knife from his hand. He had been bent over trying to get the blade out of his pocket and had it open to do me in. To this day, I'm thankful that the crowd that held us apart was not four seconds late.

The first person I saw the next morning told me I was in trouble. "You whipped the Jackson's Hole bully and he's not happy about it," he said. Down at the general store, Mr. Gabbey, the store's owner, said the same. Mr. Gabbey was a man who could be trusted and one who did not speak idly.

He told me something about John Emery. Once, during a poker game, someone had pulled a pistol on John and had shot his hat off. John had wrestled the man down, taken his pistol away from him, stuck it in the man's mouth, and pulled the trigger. When John discovered there were no more live shells in the gun, he knocked the guy on the head with the pistol and bit part of his ear off, which had to be sewn back on by Dr. Huff.

Nobody in Jackson's Hole, not even the deputy sheriff sent to the dance hall to keep order and to referee ordinary cowboy fights, had been willing to challenge John after he had slugged Dorothy. "You're somewhat of a hero in the valley," Mr. Gabbey said. "Everyone's talking about how that damn mountain climber whipped John Emery."

"I didn't really whip him," I said. "I got in a lucky blow and knocked him over the banister."

"I hear he had his knife out when they separated you," Mr. Gabbey said. "You're damn lucky to be alive. But now John has said openly that he's going to kill you on sight, and you'd better get out of the country if you want to stay alive. Paul, you've got to take this seriously. I know John Emery, and he'll do exactly what he says he's going to do. He'll kill you if you stay around and this is not settled."

Then Mr. Gabbey went in the back room and came out with his pistol. "I'm giving you this and here's some cartridges," he said. "You'd better load them and go out and practice a couple of rounds so you know how to use it. You'd better carry it with you at all times. And if you ever come near John Emery and he makes a move, you'd better shoot first. I think you're legally justified in doing so, because he's telling everyone there's not room in this valley for the both of you — and you're going to be the one who leaves quickly, dead or alive."

I didn't know what to do, but I did take the pistol. And I did shoot a few rounds to try it out and I did stick it in my pocket. That Saturday night I decided I wasn't going to keep hiding out at Jenny Lake. I was going to Jackson and if John Emery was there, I would have a showdown with him.

My first stop in town was at an old bar that was frequented by dudes from the Bar BC Ranch where John was working. I walked in unnoticed and saw John down at the dice table gambling with a group of dudes. I was nervous as hell, but I had to put on a good act. I had to sound as tough as he was. I didn't hesitate. I walked right down and touched John on the shoulder and said, "Hello, John."

"It's you," he said. "It's that mountain climber."

"Yes, that's right," I said. "I hear that you're going to kill me on sight and I'd better get out of the country if I want to stay alive. All I want to do is hear you say that once again, because the moment you do, I'm going to blow your guts out."

"You goddamn sonofabitch," he said. "Hell, there's no use fighting anymore. Come on over to the bar and let's have a drink."

Keeping my hand on my gun, I walked over to the bar and had a few drinks with him. He was very friendly. I think he was glad to settle our differences, because he was receiving some criticism for making such open threats about killing me. After that I was a little cautious when I saw John, but we would always buy each other a drink and we eventually became friends.

I wondered if I had been oversold on the ferocity of the Jackson's Hole bully. But after I had left the area that fall — when I wanted to — a cowboy friend of mine, Fernie Hubbard, began to date Dorothy. One night Fernie was staying in a one-room cabin near where the Wort Hotel is now located in Jackson. He was standing in front of the looking glass shaving when the door opened behind him and John Emery shot him twice in the back without warning. He was taken to the hospital and teetered between life and death, but finally survived.

John was thrown in jail, but that night he kicked out the roof of the jail and escaped out to Spring Gulch near the Lucas ranch. Stealing a horse and an extra rifle, he headed off into the hills for parts unknown. Posses searched everywhere, but he was never found. John Emery had disappeared from Jackson's Hole.

Shortly after he recovered, Fernie Hubbard married Dorothy Redmond and they moved to Montana, where they bought a ranch and raised a family. Some years later, John appeared one evening at one of the local bars in Jackson. It had been so long that people greeted him and asked where he'd been. John told stories of how he had dodged the posses and made it to DuBois, where they had not yet heard of his crime.

When he got to Bill Ringer's ranch up the north fork of the Wind River he had traded his horse for a fresh one and some extra food. He had been holing up in Montana ever since. Then John disappeared again. Rumor has it that he killed a man in Montana, and they strung him up.

Without realizing it, John Emery had done me a favor. Not being a native, I was always trying to establish myself in Jackson's Hole. My guiding service helped, and I was seriously thinking about developing a dude ranch. But my fight with John accomplished more than both of those things. It bought me an insurance policy in Jackson's Hole.

Years later I met an old cowboy in the Silver Dollar Bar at the Wort Hotel who started to talk about this incident, not knowing that I was Paul Petzoldt. "One thing that happened after that fight," he said, "was no other local cowboys ever asked that mountaineer to step outside."

I thought that was the end of the John Emery saga, but last year, when I was eighty-five years old, I came out of a service at the Episcopal Church in Jackson and ran into Dorothy Redmond Hubbard. My eyes don't work as well as they used to, so I didn't recognize her. But she introduced herself to me. She told me she had recently spent an evening with friends recounting the time when I protected her honor and whipped John Emery up at the dance hall.

"Dorothy," I said, "when I invited John Emery out to fight I wasn't aware of his reputation or I would never have tried to defend your honor."

CHAPTER THIRTEEN

FROM WYOMING TO WINDSOR CASTLE

"I have never let my schooling interfere with my education."
— *Mark Twain*

Late in the summer of 1933, Prentice Gray, a Wall Street banker who owned a ranch in Jackson's Hole, told me he had a guest coming from England who liked to hike every day. I took it from his tone that the gentleman was an important guest. Prentice wanted to hire me to guide him on hikes while he was visiting. I would have the use of Prentice's Model A Ford, which had just replaced the Model T, to take the Englishman up to the Tetons or anywhere else he desired to go for an afternoon walk.

The guest turned out to be Sir Albert Victor Baille, Dean of St. George's Chapel at Windsor Castle, and private chaplain to the king and queen of England. The dean and I hit it off well. I think he was a little shocked that a local Wyoming "packer and guide" was able to discuss, on his level, a variety of worldly topics, from Fascist Italy to philosophy. Our talks were always friendly, but sometimes they ended in civil disagreements. I remember one day when, to emphasize a point, the dean hit his cane over a nearby log and broke it. He told me it had been his favorite cane for twenty years.

In England, it was customary for the dean to have a drink in the evening. So once again I called on the owner of the Cash Creek still and bought some of his best stock. I delivered the moonshine to the dean regularly, sealed in a Mason fruit jar and wrapped in a brown paper bag. On his last day, just before the dean was to go by automobile to Salt Lake and then on to Hollywood, I gave him a going-away present of two quarts of the best that Cash Creek could offer.

Near the end of the climbing season that year, I received a letter from Sir Alfred asking if I would be his guest at Windsor Castle in England. He saw it as an opportunity for me to continue my studies. I think maybe in the back of his head the dean thought that, with education, maybe I would decide to take my interest for humanity and my feelings for the disenfranchised, the underdog, and the unemployed into the religious field. He saw the possibility of my using my imagination and feelings in a religious way. I knew I couldn't do that because it wasn't part of me, but I saw that if I wanted to go that way I had the opportunity, probably, for almost immediate success.

I was surprised and elated at the prospect of visiting Windsor Castle with the opportunity to meet some of the leaders of England and maybe of Europe too. I was more excited about the trip than even the possibility of climbing Everest. I wondered how the Jackson's Hole packer and guide would mix with the English aristocracy. One thing I was sure I would not do was try to ape the English, as many of our stupid, rich entrepreneurs were doing by buying estates in England, shooting in the pheasant drive, and riding to the hounds.

In his letter, the dean inquired whether I had enough money to make the trip. I was low on funds but I knew I could ride the rails almost to New York, where a friend promised to send me a little money. I would have to find the rest of the money myself for the boat ride across the Atlantic, because I wasn't going to ask the dean for any handouts.

It was tough getting into big cities like New York riding the rails. The freight trains would stop way out on the edge of the city, so it was a long ways getting into town. The passenger trains went into huge depots where there were policemen, and you were conspicuous if you got off a train with a soot-covered face.

It was also difficult getting out of the big cities on passenger trains. You had to have a ticket to get through the gates and out on the platforms where the trains were. In Chicago, I bought a cheap ticket for a train out to the suburbs. On the same platform were trains being loaded that were going further out. That's the way I got on the top of *Twentieth Century Limited* out of

Chicago. I rode it as far as Toledo. I took a bus all the way from Toledo into New York.

When I got into New York, I checked into an inexpensive hotel and washed out my socks and underwear, shaved, and got the soot out of my hair and the cinders out of my ears. I went to the American Express and got my baggage and went back to my hotel. I came out looking fairly respectable, like a human being.

I hadn't met the sons of Teddy Roosevelt in Jackson's Hole, but I knew about Roosevelt's experiences out West. I knew other Roosevelts had been to Jackson's Hole and I knew they owned a steamship line. So that was a natural place to go. I went to see the vice president of the U.S. Lines Company, Kermit Roosevelt. I told his secretary I was from Jackson's Hole and I wanted to see Mr. Roosevelt. She went into his office and came right out and said, "Go on in."

He introduced himself and I introduced myself. He had visited Jackson's Hole plenty of times with his father on hunting and fishing trips and had heard of me. He immediately asked what he could do for me. I told him the story about the dean and being invited to England. I told him I was too proud to tell the dean I didn't have the money to go, so I wanted to work my way over to England if I could.

"It's practically impossible to get you a job to go over there. There are unions to consider and your inexperience. It's not practical," he said. Then he asked me if I had a passport. I said yes, and showed it to him. Checking his schedule, Mr. Roosevelt saw that a ship was leaving for England the next day. He said, "You go out and show your passport to my secretary, and we'll see what we can do."

The secretary made some phone calls and had me wait. She asked if I could be prepared to go the next morning. I said yes. She gave me directions to the dock, where I would find the ship, the *American Farmer*. She told me to show the people down there my passport; she'd made arrangements and I'd be taken care of.

When I did that the next day, they knew who I was. They took me immediately on the ship and put me up in a room. It was a freighter with a certain number of accommodations. But my big surprise came that evening when I came down to the dining room for dinner and was shown to the captain's table. For dinner that night, and every night of the crossing, I ate with the captain.

We were not far out of the city when we hit the big storm. Boy, that was a severe storm. It delayed the trip by about three days. I thought we were going under and I think the captain was a little worried. Most days I rode in the bridge where I could watch the front of the ship go over a wave, plunge its nose into the base of a huge oncoming cliff of water, and rise up again, decks awash with seawater. Some of the ship's passengers did not emerge from their quarters until we docked near London. When I did see them for the first time they looked green and exhausted.

I was met by a distinguished gentleman wearing dark knickers, black socks, and dark shoes with bows on them. Not being used to this type of dress, I didn't recognize the dean at first, but he quickly took me in tow and we drove to Windsor Castle in his chauffeured car. I was given a room in the old part of the deanery that the dean said was built before 1500.

I had already decided that I didn't want to attend a university, and the dean accepted this. He knew that my interests in Europe were economic and political ones, and I told him I thought I could learn more by observing the people and events than by sitting in a classroom. It was also my intention to do some traveling and hopefully to climb in the Alps, so I didn't want to be tied down by going to school.

It was a fascinating time for me. The prince of Wales and several European diplomats were among the dean's dinner guests during my stay, and I was able to meet and talk with them all. The dean was also active in the theater, often being asked to critique opening-night performances and to give suggestions to directors. Once I was invited to tag along. We stayed at the Garrick Club in London and attended a show called *The Gay Divorcée*. After the show, the dean and I dined with the stars of the show, Fred Astaire and Claire Luce.

Exclusive boat trips on the Thames, the queen's garden parties, and watching the horse races from the royal box at Ascot were all part of my English experience; quite a switch from the mountain guide's life in Wyoming.

Of all the pastimes available to me, the one I enjoyed most was golf. East of Windsor Castle, meandering through the old oak trees, was the private nine-hole golf course for the king and queen. I had access to the course and often played with the poor knights, the great war heroes who didn't end up with their own fortunes and were given apartments in the walls of Windsor Castle. I always laughed when I arrived at the ninth green to see a guide showing American tourists around the porch of Windsor Castle with its view of the course. They probably thought I was Duke So-and-So instead of Paul Petzoldt from Jackson's Hole.

While visiting the dean's brother in Scotland I was able to play at St. Andrews golf course, where the British amateur championship was won that year by an American, Lawson Little. During my round there, I disgraced myself by slicing one of my drives off the course onto some nearby railroad tracks.

One day I was playing on my own at a public course not far from Windsor. I was paired with a young man who was a good golfer. He bested me, and I was only about two or three strokes out of the big time then. I told him I was playing at Stoke Poges the next day with two other golfers and asked if he would be interested in being the fourth. At that time I was reminded again of English class differences. "Oh no," he said. "I can't do that. Those men are gentlemen."

Similar incidents spurred me to plan a trip to London, where I wanted to experience life as an unemployed homeless person on the street. I allowed myself just the amount of money people on the dole were getting, which worked out to be a little over one American dollar a day. It was possible to exist on the dole if you had no other income, but I had to get a bed in one of the cheapest flophouses in the city, where I roomed with fifteen other people. None of them liked fresh air.

I took with me a cup, a spoon, and a small teapot. In nearly all the flophouses there were small coal fireplaces on the floor for heating tea water. For meals, I bought fish and chips and other inexpensive foods on the street. It was a very foreign country to me — even the dialect was hard for me to understand.

I got an idea of how desperate it was for the homeless in England then as well as in America. It was 1934, the height of the Depression. My relatives were victims of the Depression, and my trip to London was in part a quest for a solution to this problem. I had read Karl Marx and all the radicals as well as listened to those who thought the people who didn't have jobs were just lazy. I knew that wasn't true, and many people who held that philosophy soon knew it too when they lost their jobs.

Soon after my return from London, I was struck with the wanderlust again. For ten dollars I bought a secondhand, three-speed English bicycle. I biked away from Windsor Castle with a small tent, a sleeping bag, and some cooking utensils tied onto the handlebars and sides of the bicycle. When I arrived at the Cliffs of Dover, I boarded a ferry to Ostende, Belgium.

My bicycle tour of Europe began in Belgium and Holland, passing the World War I battlefields where my second oldest brother, Louie, had almost lost his life in the trenches near Liège.

As I headed down the Rhine toward Switzerland, I bicycled through Germany. Nothing I had read about Hitler and the Nazis prepared me for what I witnessed there. Every evening I saw Germans going through maneuvers, marching through their villages with sticks and sometimes actual rifles on their shoulders. "Heil Hitler" could be heard over the treetops. Every store I entered, I was met with the hand salute and "Heil Hitler." I got a little tired of saying "Heil Hitler" so I substituted "Hi, Toots."

In every shop window was a picture of Hitler, and outside a German flag often flew. I only knew a few food words in German, but I met a butcher who had lived in America and spoke English. He told me he had returned to his homeland to aid in the fight for freedom since Germany had been devastated and castrated by the Allies' peace agreements after World War I. He asked me when we were going to take care of those Jews in New York.

The Matterhorn was my objective. I wanted to see the famous mountain that Whymper had written about, and climb it. So I cut across France and went up the Rhône Valley to Fiesch and from there to Zermatt. Sometimes I would catch rides behind lorries, which weren't very powerful in those days and climbed hills rather slowly. The drivers didn't seem to mind when I hung on to the back of their trucks up the steep grades. I think it was common practice for bikers then.

There was no road from Fiesch to Zermatt, only a hiking path. Since I didn't want to spend what little money I had on a train ticket, I went mountain biking with my three-speed. Sometimes I could ride and sometimes I had to push. It was about thirty-five miles.

When I arrived in Zermatt I left my bicycle with Bernard Bernard, a famous climber and guide. We had shared some of the same clients, so he knew who I was. First I climbed Mount Rosa, the second highest peak in Europe, an easy climb, and then some of the other peaks.

Then with my pack, sleeping bag, and tent I started for the Hornli Ridge on the Matterhorn. When I woke up in the crowded hut the next morning, I had a good-looking restless girl on one side and a garlic-eating Italian on the other. Many people had already left for the top, and I wondered why they had started so early. I found out later that it was because the guides wanted to get up and down with enough time to spare to meet the train and round up more customers. I decided to wait for daylight.

It was icy on the mountain that day, and on my way up I passed many retreating parties. My attention was split between the mountain and the people, especially the Swiss guides. They did everything for their clients and didn't try to teach them anything, as I insisted my guides do in the Tetons. We would try to teach people how to climb by themselves, but the Swiss guides figured that would be bad for business. People wouldn't need guides if they knew how to climb.

On my descent, out of habit, I kept track of the other parties on the mountain. The last party was having some trouble, and I waited to see if they were going to make it down. The mountain was in bad shape and a bitterly cold wind was blowing. Finally, I knew I would have to race down if I wanted to make it back to my tent before dark, but the party I was watching was making slow progress. I doubted they could get down the difficult part of the mountain before nightfall. They didn't know how to belay, and they were tired and climbing dangerously. I thought that they would probably die if they had to spend the night on the mountain.

As I approached the party I saw that it was two men and a woman, and they were desperate. Unable to speak their language and with no time to try, I silently communicated my intention to help them. They accepted my offer, and I began to lead them down as quickly as they could travel. It was obvious, though, that we weren't going to make it to the hut before nightfall.

Without lanterns, it was impossible to climb in the dark. Luckily, I had brought along a big bivouac sac that was large enough for the four of us to huddle underneath. Well, almost all of our parts fit under the sac. We had to keep rotating during the night so everyone could get some air. None of us slept, but that was all we could do to keep from freezing to death.

At daybreak, I brought them down to the ridge that led to the hut. They tried to give me money, but I wanted sleep more, so I said no. Then I went out to my tent on the glacier and was sound asleep in seconds. It was about one o'clock that afternoon when I was awakened by a man's voice outside my tent, asking me to come out. The man was Dan Bryant from New Zealand and he was looking for a climbing partner.

The party I had rescued had been telling stories about me, how I was a miracle and had saved their lives. Dan had also heard I was a guide in the Tetons, and from his conversation assumed I was a good rock climber.

Snow and ice were his specialty since that was what most of the climbs in New Zealand were, and he said he thought we'd make a good team. He was good enough that he didn't need a guide, but he didn't want to climb alone. I was glad to have the company. So after visiting Zermatt for supplies we returned to my tent. Dan hadn't climbed the Matterhorn yet, so we decided to do a traverse and spend the night in the Italian hut.

I convinced Dan that we didn't have to start out at three o'clock in the morning like everyone else, so at first light the next day we began our traverse. Dan was a talented and fast climber, so we made good time. We passed a dead man on top who had been caught in a severe storm that had swept the mountain the day before.

We were hustling and by one o'clock had arrived at the Italian hut. The hut was trashed and it smelled like an outdoor toilet. Apparently, during the storm people had neglected to go outside to relieve themselves. There was no way we could sleep there. We still had some daylight, so we talked about continuing down into Italy.

"If we go down to Italy," Dan said, "that will be a couple of days at least and I'd like to do some more climbing with you before you leave."

Our only other option was to go back over the Matterhorn. We zoomed to the top and passed the dead man again. It was late that afternoon by the time we reached the Swiss hut. It was more crowded than usual because of the guides who had come up to help evacuate the body the next day. We didn't want to stay in the hut anyway, so we kept going for Zermatt. There we finally found what we were looking for: a good camp and good food.

It was a tremendous accomplishment, and our story was written up in the *London Alpine Journal*. The article called me an intrepid, impecunious, expert mountaineer. I had to look those words up in the dictionary to see what they meant. When the Zermatt guides got wind of the climb they took us in as brother alpinists and advised us about other challenging climbs in the area.

Dan went on to a distinguished mountaineering career that was cut short by a fatal car accident. He was one of the key players in the English attempts to climb Mount Everest that culminated in Sir Edmund Hillary's first ascent in 1953. As a boy, Hillary had been taken on his first alpine trip by Dan in New Zealand.

My money was running out, but I knew I would have some waiting for me at the Rotterdam American Express, enough to get me back to the United States. I just had to get there. I biked and camped my way to Holland, borrowing what food I could from the farmers' fields. The grapes were ripe. When I arrived at the Dutch border, however, I hit a snag. Customs officials wouldn't let me enter the country without a ten-dollar duty fee on my bike, which would be refunded when I left the country with the bike. When I explained to them that I had money waiting for me in Rotterdam and I could pay the fee then, they weren't sympathetic.

I was at a loss as to what to do, but then I remembered a band of gypsies I had passed a few miles back. After finding out what a train ticket to Rotterdam cost, I rode back and sold my bike to the gypsies. I haggled for enough money to pay for my train ticket and a good meal too.

CHAPTER FOURTEEN

THE FIRST WINTER ASCENT OF THE GRAND

"A chill no coat, however stout,
Of homespun stuff could quite shut out,
A hard, dull bitterness of cold,
The coming of a snow-storm told."
  — *John G. Whittier, "Snow–Bound"*

During the years after my first ascent of the Grand Teton, I did visit Jackson's Hole in the winter on several occasions. To get into the valley, I caught a ride from Victor over Teton Pass on the canvas-covered mail sled that came complete with a working woodstove in back. Passengers sat on either side of the sled on padded benches under which was stored the wood for the stove. It was a surprisingly comfortable ride.

The sled's first stop in the valley was Wilson, where Mike Yokel and his family operated an informal inn. Sometimes, with a new team of horses, the sled continued the nine miles on into Jackson. Some sleds were strictly freight sleds, delivering to the snowed-in, year-round natives much-needed provisions and items ordered from the Montgomery Ward catalog. Once I came over on a freight sled, sitting in front with the driver, because there was no room in back. We had to dress warm.

In the valley, practically the only way to get around was on skis or sleds in places like Teton Pass, where traffic and horses' hooves packed down the snow. Coming over Teton Pass, the runners of a sled could be on hard-packed snow three feet above the ground. Some roads were kept open, but they weren't dependable.

Paul Petzoldt studies a crevasse on the Teton Glacier. (Teton County Historical Center)

By 1935, I had purchased a small two-hundred-acre ranch on Ditch Creek, east across the valley from the Grand Teton. For the land, three cabins, a barn, and a couple of horses I paid the terrific sum of seventy-five hundred dollars. When I visited the ranch in winter, I took the sled part of the way, but it was still necessary to ski several miles from the post office at Kelly. Sometimes we didn't even bother with the sled and skied all the way from Wilson, putting up in a neighbor's ranch along the way if we couldn't make it in one day.

In the course of studying the mountains to develop my guide service I naturally thought about skiing trails. My closest friend in the valley at that time was Fred Brown, a direct descendant of John Brown, the Civil War revolutionary. The Browns owned a dude ranch south of Wilson. Fred was an imaginative person and a good skier. When I spent winters in Jackson's Hole he taught me the tricks to skiing.

My first pair of skis were homemade from straight unknotted pieces of lodgepole pine shaved down on both sides, resulting in straight-grained pieces of wood, each about the size of a ski. Skis were long, sometimes over eight feet, for better weight dispersion to keep us on the surface of the powdery snow. To curve the ski, the front end was placed in boiling water or steamed and then clamped in a curved position as it cooled.

Wax was not readily available in those days, so one of the first questions any skier would ask another if they met on the trail was "How are they running today?" The answer could be anything from smooth to sticking. But Fred was excellent at making his own wax using honey, pine tar, or axle grease. We had about four different kinds of wax for the different types of skiing conditions we encountered.

To make bindings, broken or worn belts from a thrashing machine or other farm machinery were used. The belts were glued or screwed into the bottom of the ski and formed into a boot shape. Sometimes rawhide was used to stitch the belts together, but it wasn't necessary. Our boots had rubber soles with cloth tops that covered the ankle and fastened in front by snaps. They were commonly called overshoes in those days and were standard equipment for outdoorsmen.

Instead of ordinary ski poles, we used a single piece of lodgepole pine that was good for rowing along through the deep snow. The pole was also used as a brake when we skied downhill. It was placed between the legs, and to slow down we pulled back on it so it dug into the snow. When we wanted to go faster, we'd push forward so the pole wouldn't drag as much. That's how we controlled our speed, but we had to be careful where the pole went between our legs. Local skiers often asked, as tailors did in those days, whether I dressed on the right or left.

When I came back from the Himalayas in 1939, I was invited to be a guest at the new Sun Valley ski resort in Idaho. The owners thought having me around skiing for a month and showing my movies from K2, the first color movies taken at high altitude, was worth enough publicity to put me up at one of their best hotels, pay me a little money, and let me ski for free. One day I demonstrated the braking technique for some people. It was a great show, but for the next couple of days I had difficulty sitting down.

Skiing was not just a hobby of mine. I was thinking about the possibility of guiding skiers into the mountains. Fred's family had bought some land and had built a ranch at the foot of Teton Pass. He often talked to me about bringing in skiers for the wintertime. He dreamed about putting up a rope lift using an old automobile engine. Skiing as a vacation activity was just catching on all over the United States, and Fred wanted to bring it to Jackson's Hole.

My brother Eldon was also in Jackson's Hole in the winter of 1935 and he, Fred, and I skied a lot together. Curly, which is what Eldon went by, had been one of the country's leading jockeys and in his heyday had earned so much money that he bought Cord cars by the pair. He had recently retired from the racetrack, where he had also been an owner and trainer; due to some setbacks, Curly was no longer wealthy.

The three of us, and one nonskier, would drive a pickup to the top of Teton Pass when the road was passable. From there, we would ski down to where we could join the road again and meet the pickup. We skied as fast as we could and some days we covered as much as twelve thousand vertical feet. This is how we learned to ski.

Buck Mountain, north of Death Canyon, had beautiful open slopes stretching way above timberline. As far as a feasible ski area, though, it didn't have much potential. It was hard to reach, there was avalanche danger, and it was inside the park boundaries. But below Buck Mountain, north of Wilson, there was one mountain that stood out. It was clearly visible from my ranch on Ditch Creek and it was obvious that it had great potential for skiing. Getting there took an early start to break trail and to climb over four thousand feet to the top. By the time we reached the bottom it was a full day.

After skiing it about four times with Fred and my brother, I was convinced that if a big ski area was ever going to be developed in Jackson's Hole, that was where it would be. I was so convinced that after the war, when I returned to Jackson's Hole with a little money, I purchased the Crystal Springs Ranch at the base of the hill for seventeen thousand dollars. It was about a two-hundred-acre ranch, including one big spring that gushed out of the mountain with enough pure water to serve a small town.

Before the sale was out of escrow at the Jackson State Bank, the man who sold me the ranch came with tears in his eyes saying his wife was going to divorce him if he went through with the sale. I reminded him that when I was at their home, his wife seemed as anxious to unload the ranch as he was, because the girls camp they ran there during the summer wasn't turning a profit. "She's a woman," he said, "so she's allowed to change her mind. Now she can't stand the fact that we've sold the place."

He offered to pay the real estate agent's fees, the bank's fees for the escrow, and to give me three thousand on top of that. I told him I couldn't make that kind of deal with a clear conscience. We were sitting at the Silver Dollar Bar in the Wort Hotel and my companion, maybe because he wanted a drink himself or maybe by clever design, ordered a couple Jack Daniel's. Soon the deal was made. He only ended up paying me two thousand dollars to help ease my conscience. I felt guilty all the way to the bank.

Later when the new ski area did open up there, I paid five thousand dollars for a small lot near the bottom of the lift. The very next summer I doubled my money on it. I suppose, as I write this, that I could not buy that lot back today for one hundred grand. Such is the history of Jackson's Hole where I dealt in land from time to time, always turning a small profit but always regretting the quick sale in the long run. Had I been more patient I might have been able to build a multimillion-dollar home in Jackson, like some of the poor people migrating there today.

***

One day Curly, Fred, and I decided we wanted to see what the top of the Grand Teton looked like in December. No one was winter climbing in those days except perhaps trappers going after martin, which fed on the abundant timber squirrels. But they never got above timberline because neither did the squirrels nor the martin. I saw this as an opportunity to expand my guiding service into an untapped market. This trip revealed many important aspects about the mountain during the winter.

I wore a pair of ski boots with three pairs of socks, a pair of waterproof wool knickers, a wool shirt, a toboggan cap, and a waterproof jacket. In my pack I carried woolen underwear, six extra pairs of wool socks, six extra pairs of mittens, a muffler, and wristlets.

Fred and I each had seven-and-a-half-foot skis and Curly, who was somewhat shorter, had seven-foot hickories. We carried four kinds of homemade wax with us for the trip. We also borrowed some fairly expensive sealskins that stretched the length of the bottom of our skis. They were attached with the fur pointing to the back of the ski so when we went forward the sealskin would slip easily over the snow, but if we started to slip backwards, the fur would catch in the snow.

We left Jenny Lake early Tuesday morning on December 17 under clear skies. The good weather was almost assured for at least two more days, but it had its drawbacks. Clear weather in Jackson's Hole meant cold weather, and that morning the thermometer in Grand Teton National Park had registered nearly 30 degrees below zero. We wondered what the temperature on the summit would be.

Owing to the powdery snow and our thirty-five-pound packs, it took us eight and a half hours to get to our timberline camp at the Petzoldt Caves in Garnet Canyon. We had only figured on that being a four-hour hike, so we were terribly fatigued. We decided to rest a day in camp and tackle the peak on Thursday. To our surprise the thermometer registered 15 degrees above zero at eight o'clock in the evening. We looked down with sympathy on the valley shivering in subzero weather.

The upper chamber of the caves was buried under several feet of snow. Tunneling to its entrance, we found it snug and dry inside, because in the fall I had left a piece of canvas hanging over the entrance to keep the blowing snow out, in anticipation of a winter climb. I had also left some firewood in there. One end of the shelter was a natural fireplace, and after we cleared the chimney of snow, we enjoyed a warm evening.

The next day Curly stayed in camp while Fred and I traveled up as far as the Lower Saddle on skis. In order to lighten our load for Thursday, we took our extra equipment and food and cached it there. We spent the remainder of the day resting and recuperating for the climb to the peak the next day.

Thursday morning, after a hurried breakfast of bread, butter, and tea, we crawled out of our warm den, mounted on skis, and rushed for the mountain. The temperature was 12 degrees above zero. The morning sun shining on the snow made the weather seem much warmer than it registered.

We climbed at a fairly steep angle in a series of switchbacks until we reached the Middle Teton Glacier that lies just below the Lower Saddle. There we made one gigantic switchback high on the side of the Middle Teton itself, then back to the highest point of the glacier on the north. After picking up our packs left the day before, we stuck our skis in the snow and took to the rocks. In order to avoid huge drifts of snow on the top of the Lower Saddle, we deviated from our summer route. Instead of going directly along the top of the Lower Saddle, we traversed north along its base on the east side where the wind had blown the ridge bare. We struck the Upper Saddle just where it intersects with the great couloir that leads to the Crawl one thousand feet above.

We found the going easy. Everywhere the rocks were as bare as in summer. All the light snow was blown into the canyon and onto the glaciers. The day was so perfect and climbing conditions so grand that we almost decided to take the difficult south side route above the Crawl. I had no doubt that climb could be made in winter, since the ridge was clear of snow.

We reached the Upper Saddle at 10:40 A.M. The thermometer registered 12 degrees above, but a stiff wind chilled us. After a council of war we decided to don all our clothes and leave our packs behind. When we got to the Belly Roll we agreed not to rope up until difficulty was encountered. Fred and Curly were both skilled climbers, and we felt that handling ropes was unnecessary. So we left the coiled rope behind and headed for the summit.

In climbing the Grand late in the season we had often been slowed by ice in the cracks and chimneys, especially above the Crawl. I was dumbfounded when we reached those cracks in December and found them completely bare of ice. I wondered how this was, since there hadn't been weather warm enough to melt the snow and ice, and if there had been, it would have refrozen further down anyway. Some scientists later told me that strong winds buffeting the Teton peaks in the fall and winter, even though they might be 10 or 15 degrees below zero, will sublimate the ice, causing it to evaporate.

This made immediate sense to me, because I realized that unwittingly I had used this principle in my everyday life. Back on the farm we hung our weekly washing out on the line to dry even in the dead of winter at minus 10. The clothes would freeze there like scarecrows but in a couple of days, we carried in our long underwear quite dry.

Without ice, the chimneys presented no difficulty. A few feet from the top we joined hands and then there we were, the first party ever to make a winter ascent of the Grand Teton.

We put our thermometer in the shade and sat down in the sunshine to enjoy the view. Yellowstone, Jackson, Leigh, Jenny, and Bradley lakes, so blue in the summer, were now like open white meadows in the black forests. We noticed at once the great extent of our visibility. The Wind Rivers appeared in such detail that we were able to trace out the canyons and identify individual peaks. The Sawtooth Mountains seemed only a few miles away. The Wasatch Range was also in plain view. The temperature at the top was the lowest recorded in our three days on the mountain, 5 degrees above zero.

It took us only two hours to descend from the summit to our camp, the fastest time we had ever made. As we descended the mountain the mercury first rose and then dropped remarkably. One thousand feet below the summit, at one-thirty, it was one degree warmer than freezing. The sun reflecting from the south slopes made the heat almost suffocating. After tea, we hurried down Garnet Canyon.

One thousand feet above the valley, at five o'clock, it was 12 degrees above zero. We could feel the cold air of the valley as we approached. One hour later as we arrived at Jenny Lake it was minus 10, a drop of 22 degrees in one thousand feet of descent!

The last mile or two over Lupine Meadows, our clothes, which had been dampened from falling in the snow, were suddenly frozen and stiff enough to hinder our skiing, and our eyes started to freeze from the melting snow and perspiration. Making it to Jenny Lake to escape from the cold was like reaching a snug harbor after sailing through a typhoon. This was the beginning of the realization that the temperature on the mountains was different than people thought. People thought the higher you got the colder it got, but that day it was the reverse.

**

It was a tough winter in 1936. I had the Ramshorn Ranch and had just gotten married. My wife Pat and I were coming in from Salt Lake to Jackson. We planned on taking a train up to Victor and then a sled over the pass. From Wilson up to the ranch, we were going to ski.

We got as far as Ashton, Idaho, and the train couldn't go any further because the branch line up to Victor was drifted over. They couldn't spare a big engine with a snowplow from the main line to clean it out.

We were told we had to wait. There was only one hotel, and every year they had an American dog derby there, trying to establish a big dog-racing reputation. The hotel was full — men and dogs. The railroad wouldn't tell us when they were going to open the road. So we took off on our skis and skied down the railroad tracks, which although covered with snow were good open places to ski. That night, we stayed at a ranch part of the way down. We arrived in Victor the next night, where we got into an old hotel that was closed up because the train wasn't bringing them any business.

The next day, we went over the pass to where Gibb Scott was living just north of Wilson. That's where we stayed for a few days, hoping the storm would go down. It was around Christmas and we had the big celebration. That's when the big cook didn't make it to her bunk one night.

At Gibb's ranch there was a main house, but most of the people who lived there stayed out in little cabins like they did on dude ranches. Long about two o'clock in the morning, the cook left the main house. There was a lot of liquor flowing, naturally. Well, when you walked back and forth to your cabin, you built up hard snow and pretty soon you had a narrow, hard trail. But off to the side, there was about four or five feet of soft snow. When the cook went out there that night, she fell off the trail. Somebody wondered if she'd gotten to her cabin all right and went to check. The cook was out in the deep snow and she couldn't get back up on the trail.

The half-inebriated group went out there and rolled around in the snow, trying to pull her back on the path. One guy was going over to the barn to get a team of horses, when Gibb reminded him, "Hell, you can't even get the horses over here. What the hell are you doing?"

Gibb had an old toboggan around, and they sort of rolled the cook onto the toboggan and held her there. Some guys got over to the porch of the cabin where they could get something to pull the rope around and they'd say, "one, two, three, heave" and "one, two, three, heave." Finally, we got her over to the cabin. I guess my wife and another woman put her to bed.

CHAPTER FIFTEEN

THE NORTH FACE

"No matter how high you are in the mountains there is always a slope going up."
  — *Ernest Hemingway, December 22, 1923*

For me, the mental part of mountain climbing was more challenging than the physical. I knew I could climb but I took pride in my route-picking. After studying a place for a while and working out the handholds and footholds in advance, I would test my routes in actuality. I'd had so much practice in my childhood on the walls of the Snake River Canyon that it was a game to me. I wasn't interested in developing a route to say I was the first to climb it. I wasn't interested in climbing some of the easy peaks just to say I was the first one up there. I didn't have that type of ambition.

I viewed mountaineering, when I was young, as noncompetitive, and it was sort of known as a great sport because of it. You didn't have to tackle anybody or hurt anybody to get to the top of a mountain. You didn't have to outrun anybody. There weren't any losers; there were just winners. That was a marvelous idea and gave everybody a wonderful feeling about climbing mountains. It was a neutral sport. If you were defeated it was because you didn't get to the top, but you didn't have to put anybody else down. You didn't have to throw rocks at somebody climbing below you so they couldn't get to the top.

***

While developing my guiding service in the early 1930s, I thought we should have a climb that was primarily over snow. There was no such climb on the Grand Teton. A snow route would help people prepare for climbing on glaciers in the

Paul silhouetted against the North Face of the Grand Teton in 1927. Photo taken by Fritiof Fryxell. (American Heritage Center, University of Wyoming)

Northwest United States. The northeast face of Mount Owen looked like the perfect route. I had looked it over from below while exploring Cascade Canyon and also from the St. John's peaks on the west side of Jenny Lake.

Big patches of snow lingered on the north side of Mount Owen all summer, turning to ice late in the season, providing a suitable place to try some climbing with crampons. Crampons were not necessary on most of the other climbs in the Tetons I had encountered up until then.

When I had a slight lull in business, I went with two of my friends up Cascade Canyon, beyond where we had started our climbing school near the falls. I was going to make the climb solo, but I needed my friends' help to cross the swollen Cascade Canyon River. Tied on to a rope that was belayed around a tree by my two friends, and holding my clothes above my head, I forded the river. It was a hot summer day, but the water was cold.

I saw this crossing as a way of making the climb more difficult for dudes. If I had to, I knew I could drop a couple pine trees across the water for a temporary bridge if the climb ever became popular, which it never did.

I was alone from then on, but most of the snow climb was of the nature that if I had fallen I could have made a self-arrest with my ice ax. I used this climb as an opportunity to test my theories about controlling my heartbeat and breathing in rhythm with my steps as a way of conserving energy. Soon I was near the top, where I skirted my way around to the west side and finished the climb as we had finished the Koven Route. I came down the same way, and it was great fun glissading the spacious snowfields using my ice ax as a rudder.

When I arrived back at the river that afternoon, the water level had dropped enough to allow me to cross it alone. Mountain-fed rivers are generally at their highest in the morning because they are carrying runoff from the day before. By the afternoon, rivers are only carrying the water that melted during the night, which is considerably less.

I never guided that climb, but I did bring people down that way, which made for an interesting traverse of Mount Owen —

going up the Koven Route from Surprise Lake and then down the snowfields to Cascade Canyon, passing the site of our guiding school, and sometimes catching a boat across the lake back to camp.

***

I spent the second longest night of my life on that side of Mount Owen. I climbed a lot with Sterling Hendricks, a friend from the Department of Agriculture. He was an agricultural scientist, and I think he worked out on their experimental farms.

Sterling and I had taken this guy up on Mount Owen. In coming down, we thought that instead of going down the regular way, where we had to descend a very steep icy couloir and use rope for safety and some rappeling to get on the Teton Glacier and over to Amphitheater Lake, it would be just as easy or perhaps easier to go down the north slope. I'd been up it by then and I knew if we glissaded down the snowfields, we could go practically right down to Cascade Creek just above Hidden Falls. From there, it was just a short walk down to Jenny Lake where we could get a boat across.

The gentleman we were with was not as good on descent as he was on going up. Climbing up the mountain and looking up, he was a pretty good climber, but his descending technique, especially on snow, was very limited. He hadn't been to the climbing school, and he was much more terrified by rappeling than we expected. He absolutely freaked out. He was so frightened of the snow it was almost impossible to make him take a step. Even though we took the faster route, we were slowed down to the point that we couldn't get off the mountain before darkness.

We had to bivouac there in the middle of the descent on a rocky ledge. We just sat there all night, freezing to death. Hendricks spent most of the night trying to explain to me various mathematical equations. He could take the Big Dipper and the North Star and the angle to tell what time of night it was without using a watch, which didn't make the time pass any quicker.

When we got down the next morning, we had to ford the river. We took off our clothes and socks and put our boots back on and laced them tight so we could ford the stream and not hurt our feet. Of course, that was rather chilly. When we got across, we took off our boots again and dried them out a little and put back on our socks and clothes. Before Hendricks and I were completely dressed, our companion had dressed and unannounced had taken off down the trail. He knew he didn't need us anymore. But we certainly knew where he went, because he had spent the last hour of the morning talking about bacon.

I cursed myself for being caught out on a second long night, which I had sworn would never happen to me as long as I climbed mountains. It wasn't a climb with one of our most pleasant endings; fortunately our client's tip was liberal.

***

I'd heard the name Fritz Wiessner long before I finally met him. He was a German living in New England who had a terrific reputation, not only as an expeditioneer in the Himalayas but also as a rock climber of unequaled skill. He was a pioneer of rock engineering, climbers I later called the five-niners. It is now known as sport climbing, which thankfully distinguishes it from mountaineering.

I met Fritz through Betty Woolsey, the captain of the American Olympic ski team and owner of a ranch in Jackson's Hole. I was invited to go climbing with them and some others whose names I've forgotten. Our objective was to climb up above Gunsight Notch and take a look at the North Ridge, previously climbed by Fryxell and Underhill.

I let Fritz take the lead and I followed, leading the second rope. It was quickly apparent that our route-picking techniques differed. Instead of switchbacking to select the easiest route between two ledges, he took it straight on, which involved unnecessarily difficult moves. I was impressed by his climbing skill, but I thought he was either trying to improve his rock climbing, impress somebody, or he was a damn poor route-finder, and I didn't feel like any of that. So as I followed with the second rope, I chose easier routes that might have annoyed him.

It took all day to reach the top of Gunsight Notch, so we only rested a short time there before we had to leave.

I met Fritz on several occasions after that and discussed with him the possibility of climbing the North Face of the Grand. I had been thinking about it ever since Fryxell had taken the picture of me from Mount Owen silhouetted against the sheer wall. Fritz said he would like to join me in an attempt, so we agreed to make a go at it before he went back East.

Some time later, I returned from a trip up the Grand fairly early one afternoon and was immediately told by my brother, Curly, who was assisting me with the guiding service that summer, that Fritz, Betty, and a few others had decided to attempt the North Face. They had left Jenny Lake that afternoon to camp at Amphitheater Lake below the Teton Glacier, and were going to try the only unclimbed side of the Grand Teton the next day.

I was disappointed and a little amused that Fritz was trying to beat me out of the honor of the first ascent of the North Face. I had a fella named Jack Durrance working for me then who was a good rock climber. Jack and his brother Dick were both on the American Olympic ski team. Jack had come to the Tetons one summer with a bunch of his friends from Dartmouth. We did some climbing together that year, and when he returned the next summer I asked him if he would assist me with some guiding as well as with the climbing school. After that Jack became one of my regular guides and a good one.

Jack and my brother enthusiastically backed the plan I hatched after hearing Fritz had secretly left for the North Face. It was after dark before we had collected our ropes and equipment. I brought along a bunch of my homemade strap-iron pitons of various thicknesses and widths. They could hold almost anything, but were sometimes difficult to remove once hammered into a crack.

Without resting, we started for Amphitheater Lake. Once there, we tiptoed past Fritz's camp and heard the slight snoring of sleeping mountaineers. We were like ships passing in the night. By daylight, we were beyond the East Ridge and on the glacier. We aimed for the first of three shelves that angle up and to the west across the North Face. Although separated by smooth cliffs, the shelves looked like the best way to the top.

I led up through the first chimney, which was overhanging at the top and was filled with a combination of ice, and loose, rotten rock. Jack belayed me through the pitons that I drove in as I climbed. He and Curly had to stand aside to avoid being hit by the rocks I knocked down. Some I accidentally dislodged, but others that I thought would be dangerous to other climbers, I threw out intentionally.

I managed to swing out of the rotten chimney onto the face, which had plenty of handholds, and climb far enough up to have a good belaying place to bring up the others. Jack took over my belaying point and belayed me up to another stance, where I could drive in another piton. Curly brought up the rear, hammering out every piton he could and carrying the heaviest pack.

Since Jack was wearing his felt-soled shoes he took the lead at this point over an extra-smooth pitch with few safe handholds or footholds. I was wearing my hiking boots, so from then on we shared the lead and made a good team. It was not extremely difficult climbing but very exposed, and protection was crucial. Soon we were on the first shelf on the perpendicular wall of the North Face.

While Jack and I kept taking turns leading, Curly continued to do the unenviable job of dangling on the end of the rope collecting pitons, since we weren't sure we were going to have enough to finish the climb. About the time we reached the second shelf, Fritz's party appeared on the glacier below. We saw them stop and point up, but they didn't yoo-hoo at us so we didn't yoo-hoo at them. We just continued on our way.

The ledges were wider than they looked from the valley. Every once in a while a rock would come whizzing down from above us, but generally they would bounce over our heads. It seemed to me there were a lot of rocks falling, but some of them turned out to be birds playing on the North Face.

Once we reached the third shelf I knew if we could get over to the North Ridge we could make it to the top, since I had climbed down to there with Sterling Hendricks in 1933. All we had to do was get around the corner. At the end of the third shelf, we found a place for a piton that enabled us to rappel down to where we would be able to get around that corner. From there, it was just a matter of following the route I had already explored three years earlier.

It was an exhilarating climb that helped us forget about our sleepless night. It had taken a long time, since we had been removing pitons as we climbed, so we didn't stay on top long. Curly was tired from carrying the heavy pack most of the way up, and Jack may have been a little worn too, but we had plenty of energy to make it down to the caves just before darkness settled in.

By then I had permanent bedding and cooking supplies stored at the caves, so we cooked up some stew and enjoyed a sumptuous meal. We fell soundly asleep still wondering what Fritz had said upon seeing us well up on the North Face when he arrived on the glacier. According to statements I've patched together since, Fritz's reaction was, "Betty, I don't think we would have liked the climb anyway. It looks too easy."

Years later, when Fritz would visit Betty Woolsey at her ranch and I would join them for dinner we often discussed the Himalayas. I had been part of an unsuccessful all-American attempt to climb K2 in 1938. I had stayed in India after the climb, hoping to be invited on the 1939 attempt that was being led by Fritz. One night I commented on the unfair treatment he had received for his role in the 1939 climb that ended in the tragic deaths of one of the party and three Sherpas. Even though he was the leader, I didn't think he should have been held entirely responsible. He didn't get a fair deal, partially because of the political climate that discriminated against Germans and partially because of rivalry in climbing circles. I was flattered when he told me that the greatest climbing mistake he had ever made in his life was not inviting me on the '39 climb. "I think, Paul," he said with his German accent, "we would have got to the top."

CHAPTER SIXTEEN

PLANE WRECK ON MOUNT MORAN

"Report of Paul Petzoldt on Mt. Moran accident, Nov. 21, 1950, submitted to the Civil Aeronautics Board Safety Bureau, Washington, D.C.: I am a part owner of the guiding concession in Grand Teton National Park and have been climbing in this area since 1924. With Mr. Blake VandeWater, I was directed by the National Park Service to locate the airplane and reach it and learn if any persons aboard were still alive. We started on Thanksgiving, Nov. 23rd, on skis and established a camp as far up the mountain as we were able to go on that day. The radio communications spotted the plane for us on the mountain as seen from the air. We directed our next day's course toward the wreckage and established a camp near timber line in rough terrain and climbed further up toward the wreckage driving in "pietons," and making a trail through the deep snow. Darkness prevented us from reaching the plane that day. The following day, we retraced our trail and with the use of mountaineering technique were able to reach the plane between 12:00 noon and 1:00 P.M. There was no sign of life or no sign that anyone had survived the crash. We took photographs of the wreckage. We found what appeared to be the partially charred remains of one unidentified person in the wreckage. No other bodies were found."
— Jackson Hole Courier, *November 30, 1950*

It was around Thanksgiving and there had been a storm over the mountains and a storm over the sagebrush plains, near Riverton, Wyoming, where I had my two bands of sheep for their winter pasture. One of the helpers from my ranch came out on a sweaty horse and told me that there was an emergency in Teton Park. I was to call the ranger immediately. He also said I had a call from the sheriff in Jackson's Hole. In a few hours, I was back to a telephone near Riverton. I first called the sheriff.

My messenger had said something about a plane on top of Mount Moran. I thought if the sheriff and the park's people were looking for me, they probably wanted my help with some sort of rescue. I certainly had no enthusiasm about climbing Mount Moran in the winter, especially on the regular routes on the east side. The east side of Mount Moran is covered with outward-slipping slabs and with vertical steps like shingles on a roof; it is a place of continuous avalanches during the winter. I considered this side of Mount Moran unclimbable in the winter.

The sheriff was John Emery's brother, Olin, who was a trustworthy and popular sheriff of Jackson for years. He did a great job of walking a tightrope in Jackson's Hole, where he had to be the upholder of law and order among the citizenry, and also tolerate, if not encourage, the slot machines and all-out, open, no-holds-barred gambling that went on and was one of the valley's best paying industries.

Well, Olin was glad to hear from me. He said, "You get over here right away. When we first heard about this plane, guys just started to jump in cars and go up there and get on their skis and start racing toward Mount Moran without any real preparation. How in the hell can they just go out there on skis with one pack and hope to get up near the top of Mount Moran where Peterson saw that light? That's impossible. It's blowing and snowing like hell and I doubt if they come back alive.

"You get your ass over here," he said. He told me I was lucky to get through to him, because the phone was ringing off the hook, day and night. Everybody all over the United States was wondering what was wrong with this sheriff in Wyoming. Why hadn't he gotten a posse together and charged up there with his horses? He said, "And this goddamn bastard down in Aspen. He's getting all that publicity in *The Denver Post* and over the TV telling them what a sonofabitch I am because I won't let him bring his dog team up here and mush out to rescue them. These people don't know what kind of country I'm in charge of up here."

Paul in a chimney on Mount Moran. Photo was taken in 1940. (American Heritage Center, University of Wyoming)

And he was right. Oh boy. You mean you're sittin' in your office and those people are dying up there on the mountain? Where's your posse? They expected a Hollywood rescue. Olin told me, "I'm going to let the park take care of this one. I told these bastards when they elected me sheriff that my authority ended at timberline."

It had never quite been decided who was in charge of the law up there in the Tetons. They didn't know whether it was the sheriff or the park. And I didn't know either.

At that time, the only transportation I had was a ton-and-a-half grain truck that had a good motor. So my wife and I got in that and went over Togwotee Pass in a blinding snowstorm. We didn't think we'd get on to Jackson, so I called Struthers Burt at his ranch nearby. He invited us to spend the night.

The next day, I drove straight into Jackson and didn't stop at the park, because I would have had to turn off at Moose and backtrack up there. I wanted to go straight on into Jackson and see what the lay of the land was and I wanted to talk to the sheriff. Also, I hoped to talk to some of the guys who had gotten back from their ill-advised charge toward the mountain and see what condition the snow was in up there. That's when I went into the cowboy bar to have a drink and heard these guys talking down at the other end. They didn't recognize me or didn't see me come in. They were talking about the plane wreck. They'd heard that I was coming over, and one of them said, "Well, my god, they got the right sonofabitch now."

That's the way they talked: "If he can't get up there, nobody can." It didn't make me feel so good, because if the plane was where they had seen the light, I knew it was atop the northeast ridge and I had climbed the northeast ridge in summertime. I knew that nobody in his right mind would climb over those slabs that were now covered with new-fallen snow.

I wasn't going up there for any amount of money. I wasn't going to commit suicide on a mountain for glory. To hell with that. I wanted to live. It wasn't worth it. It was too dangerous.

But then, I thought later, that money or no money I was hooked. I'd have to make an attempt to get up there. I'd made my living in Jackson's Hole. I'd established my reputation in

Jackson's Hole. I'd come from being an unknown kid to a person who was recognized. Here and now I could see that the people in Jackson's Hole expected me to get up there. It would have been damn hard for me to say no.

I talked things over with the sheriff and learned the terrific thing that had happened. The plane was full of religious missionaries who were willing to sacrifice their lives, as their predecessors had, in going to new tribes that had never heard the word of God. That's why it was called New Tribes Mission, because they wanted to go with the Bible and the word of God to tribes who had never heard about it before. From a media standpoint, what more could you have? So there was terrific interest in every newspaper, every radio, all over the country. And they kept the phones in Jackson's Hole jammed.

The sheriff also told me the military were involved in a rescue attempt. They had already sent a crew over the Tetons, who were planning on parachuting out to rescue any survivors. Of course, they couldn't see down through the clouds. Luckily they didn't jump, or we would have been looking for them yet.

***

I had never made a winter rescue before except in the ski troops. We did some doozies there. We went up a mountain — it was about 15 degrees below zero in the wind at night — to bring a sentry with appendicitis of some sort off the mountaintop where he shouldn't have been, even in war. I had developed the original techniques of mountain evacuation and winter mountain-evacuation in the ski troops, so at that time I knew perhaps as much about it as anybody.

But when I went up to the park, I didn't want to lay down the law. I was hoping that they would give me the leadership of the situation and not give the leadership to somebody in the army or in the park service or something like that. When I met them up there that happened almost immediately.

The park superintendent and the chief ranger said to me, "We're going to put you in charge. Will you accept the responsibility?"

"Jackson Lake isn't frozen over yet, but there's plenty of snow on the mountain," I said. "I want boats over there and I want the army team that's here to stay and support us." I said if Blake will go with me, I want Blake, because he is a park ranger and a climber. We agreed, and they got everything I needed to go the next morning.

Blake VandeWater was about my age, maybe a little younger. He had married one of the Simpson gals. Well, maybe Blake wasn't married then, but later on he married and he left the park service. Simpson was a hardware man in town, and Blake became the head of the hardware store there in Jackson.

Since Jackson Lake was open, there was no use skiing from the roadhead like those fellas had, miles up there to the base of Mount Moran. The road went up to the dam at Moran, and along there we caught a boat that took us across the lake and dropped us off right there at the base of the mountain. We wanted to get to timberline and see how the weather developed and be ready to make plans from there. That was about as far ahead as we could plan, because we thought we knew where the plane was, but we weren't absolutely sure. If it was over on another ridge, further to the south, it could have been a different thing.

We skied and carried stuff up to timberline. Army people broke the trail through the snow for us and carried loads up to our first camp. I wasn't going to let Blake and me break the trail; we needed to save ourselves.

Before we left I got two copies of a picture of Mount Moran and drew lines across vertically and horizontally and numbered each one of the small squares, from one to about fifty, and gave one copy to the park people and I kept the other one. They could give their copy to the people who were flying over. If they saw the plane wreck, then all they would have to do would be to tell us the plane was in square thirty-four and we would know exactly where it was. That's why when the search plane flew over and the clouds broke we knew exactly where to find the plane. It was below the summit practically right on top of the northeast ridge. That meant we were going to go over very dangerous avalanche country during most of the loop.

We built a fire at our camp at timberline. I wondered if any passengers were alive, and wondered about how it was up there. Of course, it had been a night or two, so there probably weren't any survivors. I didn't expect there to be. The mountain was practically invisible from the blizzard and the howling wind. Every once in a while we heard avalanches come down. I worried about the terrific chance we were taking.

Our radio wasn't working that first night, but eventually Jim Huidekoper brought us a replacement. We learned over the radio that they had spotted the plane. They told us where we could find it on the grid.

The next morning, early, Blake and I got in all our climbing gear. For a ways we had army guys still breaking our trail. We were on skis for a while. Then we were on rock and snow. It took a lot of effort and a lot of caution because sometimes we were waist-deep in snow and had to step up on the rocks. We possibly could have used snowshoes, but it was awfully deep. The army people took us up as far as where the rock climbing started. Then they left us there, and we went on up.

That's when we got into the real climbing; we had to. Blake and I took turns leading, but we didn't get very far because we had to put pitons in the rock. It was very steep there for a ways. We were trying to keep off the ledges, but we couldn't. We managed to deliberately avalanche one ledge so we could get some more pitons in, but it was getting late by then.

There was no ice. In the winter by the time it starts to snow, there's less ice than there is in the fall, even down low. That was one of the difficulties. The snow was not frozen to those rocks. It would slide right off, especially since it was powdery snow. It was new snow and it wasn't very stable. It was very dangerous. We only got started that second day.

When we came down, we didn't want to go back to where our camp had been before and have to climb up through the deep snow the next day. We radioed down to Jim Huidekoper and some of the army rescue workers and others who were maintaining our lower camp to bring up our camping equipment and some food so we would stay at the base of the cliff for the night. Huidekoper, who figured very prominently in the rescue effort as the liaison between us and the park service, led the group to bring our tents, sleeping bags, and some food. We were about one thousand feet above the original camp, and about two thousand feet below the plane at this point.

The next morning after a little breakfast, as soon as it was light, we started for the plane again. We used the pitons we'd put in the day before and, gradually proceeding, swept the snow away or avalanched the snow away, trying to get to cracks in the rock where we could put in more pitons.

Blake was a wonderful climber, great. He was perfect, because he had the authority of the park and could make a report and take that responsibility. I would have hated to take on the responsibility of making an official report back to the park service, because they had to answer to all those people throughout the world, relatives and friends and people who didn't understand the situation.

When we got near the wreck, there was one big snowfield we had to cross. We could see the crows around up by the plane. Well, hell, crows find meat. We yoo-hooed and we didn't get any answer. Of course, we didn't know yet whether anybody might still be alive.

There was this last place that we had to cross, a big ledge, and there was no place to put in pitons. It was either turn back or cross it. I went up that thing very carefully. The first thing that happens in an avalanche is the snow starts to settle and, boy, I was listening for that sound. We crossed over it without an avalanche.

***

The hull was empty, and scattered around were pieces of cloth and baggage and the remains of some people. I had never seen a plane wreck before and I didn't know what a plane wreck could do, especially when a plane hit a solid wall. The back end of the plane was there, but when you looked inside the fuselage there was nothing. There was no wiring, no seats, no boards. Nothing but aluminum. The rest of it had gone right out through the front of the plane. One wing was gone off the plane; there was a place where it could have gone around the rock. The wing has never been found. Whether it's buried under the glacier or not, no one knows.

We didn't see much. Maybe some of the bodies were covered with snow, but I think that when the plane went through there an avalanche took them onto the glacier way below. The biggest body part we found on the surface was a torso with missing parts. Everyone was undoubtedly killed immediately when they went out with the flying debris and the engine parts against the rocks.

I wasn't conscious of all of the stuff Blake found, but we picked up any papers and took them down to the park. We spent quite a bit of time around the wreck, about an hour, just looking it over. Blake was making notes to report to the park service. I was very anxious to get down.

We went back, stepping in the exact footprints we had come up, and luckily that upper slab didn't avalanche. When we got down to our pitons we felt pretty safe. Climbing, holding on to the rope, maybe doing a little rappeling, we got safely down to our sleeping bags and our little tent. I think we started at daylight and got to the wreck around one or two o'clock so we'd have enough time to get down. I was scared to death. It was snowing and not snowing, and snowing and not snowing, not real cold but cold enough to freeze. We stayed that night at our high camp and reported by radio.

We said that there should be no attempt to rescue the bodies. We thought for sure it couldn't be done without further loss of lives. I didn't say publicly that there weren't any bodies, but we told the park service the situation. They phoned the people of the New Tribes Mission, and by the next day they announced the decision that there would be no further rescue attempts.

I was saddened, but I had anticipated it. I didn't see how anyone could have survived the wreck, much less the nights that followed. It would have been miraculous. It happens in the movies, but the movies are not always reality.

That ended the thing, except that I had mentioned that I had given lectures at Chico University, and that I'd met members of this New Tribes Mission. Although I wasn't a missionary type myself, I thought that if you're in favor of missionaries, these people were somewhat like heroes in attempting to risk their lives to bring the Bible and the word of God to tribes that had never heard it before. This was one of the principles of the Christian religion that they believed in.

I didn't know anyone on the plane, but I'd met the New Tribes' leader. I'd talked quite a bit to him. He was a very interesting, dynamic person, as you would have to be to organize and do this work. Some of them associated me with the religion because I'd spoken friendly of it. There was even somebody who came up with the idea, a strange idea, that maybe the crash wasn't in vain, because they had sort of found me, who could help them carry on their religion. Of course, I was sympathetic to these people, but suddenly they thought I was a member of the mission and started to treat me as such. That embarrassed me.

They were calling me and writing to me that they were glad that I had the same faith that they did and believed in the principles that they did, and I could be of great help to them in the future. They were just going to take me right in. It's no more wild than some religious things. Today, knowing cults and religions and how they operate sometimes without any rhyme or reason I can see how this sort of thing was possible. But back then it was a development that I never in my dreams imagined might take place.

Later, *The Mountain*, a movie with Spencer Tracy, really tainted the rescue attempt. The story was about a plane wreck on a mountain. Spencer Tracy played this crack guide who climbed to the crash with his little brother. The kid was greedy and stole some money from the wreck and got his comeuppance. Justice was done when he fell in the crevasse with his loot, never to be seen again. The movie came out six years after the Mount Moran wreck. When it did rumors started to get around that there was a lot of money on that plane and I'd brought it down with me and hadn't told anyone. That grew like a fish story. Suddenly, I think almost everybody in the country believed that I had gotten a few thousand dollars out of there and brought it down, but I didn't fall in a crevasse along the way.

That haunted me all my life. Just last year, in my old age, after going over Teton Pass I stopped at the Stagecoach Inn at the bottom of the hill like I generally do, because it's the one place still frequented by old-timers. I went in there and there was an old old-timer sittin' there and he bought me a Jack Daniel's. He sat me down and he said, "Paul, you old sonof-abitch, now you can finally tell me the truth. How much money did you get out of that plane?"

***

Of course, when we went up the next summer after the wreck we didn't find money either. After the snow melted, we had two doctors from Wyoming go up to sign death warrants. There were also some aeronautics people who wanted to look over the plane and try to find out the reason for the crash, and a couple of people from the New Tribes Mission. I think Blake was along too, and I had Glenn Exum go along to help. The people in the New Tribes Mission would identify a suitcase or a piece of cloth or something like that, and that would be enough for the doctors to sign death warrants so that estates could be settled and all that sort of thing.

I was looking around in the rocks where there were these little sort of oyster shells. I thought, well, there's igneous rock here, but up on the top they have these caps of the original sea bottoms that were here before the mountain was uplifted. That's why Mount Moran has these two flat tops, because they're crowned with these old sea bottoms and they're full of little shells and things. But then I looked at them closely and I thought, my god, these are pieces of skulls. And maybe baby skulls.

Just before we left, I looked up into a crack where the snow hadn't melted yet. It looked like there was a shoe up there, and I had to have somebody boost me up there so I could reach the shoe. It was solid and we dug it out. Here was the aviator, his whole body. His head was a little mushy but he had his clothes on. He had a billfold in his pocket, and papers and so forth. We did with him as we had with the other remains. We put some rocks over him. They had a little burial ceremony there with the ministers from the New Tribes Mission.

The park people said they didn't have any money to pay me for this. They offered me park wages for the extra help. I don't know what that was — maybe two or three dollars an hour. I said, I don't want that. They said, we've called Washington, D.C., and the Department of the Interior said it wants to give you the highest award it can give, and that's the Conservation Award. It was for my leadership and going up and getting to the plane. Blake got it too.

The park closed that ridge for climbing for a year or so. I don't know whether the park sent some rangers up there to cover up the remains of bodies. But, of course, over time they're all picked clean by the crows and ravens.

CHAPTER SEVENTEEN

TALON FINGERS
AND WILD EYES

"Human beings are the funniest people."
— *Paul Petzoldt*

Guiding was a wonderful way to learn about people and what their real feelings were. The reality of hikes and climbs generally brings out the real person. They're not bluffing and "they ain't being something they ain't," as they say in Jackson. Of course, we had all types.

I especially liked taking natives up, because I saw them getting enthused about something they never thought possible for them to do. They never considered climbing the Grand Teton, because it wasn't socially or culturally acceptable to the local population. It was terrible to waste your time doing something like that. What could you bring back from the top of the mountain: maybe a little pebble or some thin air? That was about all. You were going out there for nothing, and that wasn't an acceptable attitude in those days. I think that was more prevalent in the West where people *worked* for a living.

There was one fella I took on some difficult climbs, and when we got into the hard parts he would talk to himself, would practically cry, and give himself hell for not being able to do certain things. It was quite annoying at first, and I thought he must be nuts. He acted like it was a terrible thing he was doing. I thought, why does he do it if he doesn't enjoy it?

We climbed Mount Moran, and I took him on the East Ridge or someplace like that. He was almost crying all the way up and all the way down, like he was suffering. He became a good friend of mine, and when we went to the bars together he was an entirely different person. I never discussed it with him, but it was crazy; he was almost insane. The other guides wouldn't take him; they wouldn't have anything to do with him. He was like a two-year-old on the end of my rope.

Another character we came across, and we used to mock this fella with his English accent, wanted to climb and he wanted his wife to go along. They were from England, and we were anxious for their business. The only problem was they had a dog with them, evidently one they had brought all the way from home. It was a very personal friend of theirs.

The Englishman wanted to climb badly but he couldn't make up his mind to go because he didn't have any place he trusted to leave his dog. There weren't any kennels, and no one who volunteered to look after the dog was satisfactory to him. Finally, someone at Teton Park headquarters who had a pen said he would take care of the dog. The Englishman investigated him and thought he would be all right. He told us time and time again he couldn't leave his dog with just anyone because she was about to come into heat and some "common" American dog might take "adVONtage" of her. He didn't want to go back to England with a bunch of pups from some common American dog.

***

I had no set fees for guiding a party up the Grand Teton, or for other climbs, but I tried to get at least fifty dollars for a climb up the Grand. If it was a group, I would charge a minimum of twenty-five dollars per person. This lack of set fees sometimes caused me some difficulty.

Dr. Frank Bartlett, his wife, and their two sons, Jay and Frank Jr., arrived one evening in the park and asked me to guide them up the Grand Teton. They told me they had been scrambling around some easy mountains in Colorado and I would have no difficulty in taking them up the Grand. Dr. Bartlett and his sons had been running long distances and were speed climbers, and his wife assured me she was in excellent shape as well. They said they didn't want to waste two days climbing. They wanted me to take them up and back in one day. So I said I would.

In 1933, Paul belays a climber from a snowy ledge about six hundred feet from the summit of the Grand Teton. (Cleve Petzoldt Collection)

We started out at three o'clock the next morning, July 15, 1933, and climbed quickly. By the time we got up to the caves, Mrs. Bartlett had lost her enthusiasm about the climb and said she didn't want to go any further. I told her to rest at the caves until we came down. The other three and I were able to reach the top with good speed and not much difficulty.

We were back at the campground before dark. It may have been the first one-day guided ascent of the Grand. The family enjoyed fast climbing and fast hiking, but their main purpose was to return home to Ogden, Utah, with a picture of the Grand Teton and to be able to say they had climbed it. They were "peak collectors," and the Grand Teton, like a hunter's prized antlers, was something they desired to have in their repertoire.

That night, Dr. Bartlett asked me how much he owed. There were four of them, so I said one hundred dollars. He almost fainted. "Why?" he said. "In Maine, I only pay the guy six dollars a day. I would gladly give you ten or fifteen. But a hundred dollars a day — that's ridiculous!"

I repeated the figure and said it didn't make any difference if it took two or three days to do it. I had taken a chance with him and raced up the Grand Teton, without enjoyment, to satisfy his wants. I thought I deserved the regular fee. He was sputtering by this time, "Ridiculous, ridiculous."

So I said, "Doctor, how much do you get for an appendicitis operation?"

"That doesn't have anything to do with it," he said. "I had to go to school and learn how to operate. I spent a lot of time learning how to do what I do."

"Well, I risked my life going up the Grand Teton when I was only sixteen," I said. "And since that time I've spent years learning how to climb. As a matter of fact, I spent much of my youth in the Snake River Canyon learning how to climb. In the past few years I've learned the technique of handling people, and how to protect them. My ability to take you up to the top of the Grand Teton and bring you back alive is just as skilled in my field as performing an operation and perhaps saving a person's life is in yours. I have people's lives in my hands every day, just like you do. If you want to be a horse's ass and not pay my hundred dollars, just go on and I'll donate my services for your climb."

It was a hard-boiled approach, but he took out his checkbook and wrote me out a check for one hundred twenty-five dollars. As he handed it to me he said, "I never thought of it that way."

I thanked him, and we shook hands and parted as friends. That argument illustrated one of the differences I wanted to establish with my guiding service. We weren't Maine guides. We weren't packers and guides who worked for a few dollars a day. We were experts who knew what we were doing and had people's lives in our hands. We deserved to be paid more than ordinary workers' wages for our expertise and for taking on the responsibility we did with every climb.

Glenn Exum, one of my guides and a good friend, also guided a party up that day. He took Cleve Petzoldt, my nephew, and fifteen-year-old Burell Bandel to the summit. Burell broke my record for the youngest climber ever to reach the peak and held that record until it was broken an hour later by Jay, thirteen, and Frank Jr., eleven.

***

One person who did not squabble over my fees was Prentice Gray, the Wall Street banker. When he had decided he wanted to climb the Grand Teton in 1932, Glenn and I had made a special effort for him because we were often guests at his ranch and his wife's ranch. I had also developed a relationship with his daughter, Barbara.

Prentice had not climbed mountains before, but he was an adventurous person who had done a lot of sailing and exploring. Of course, being president of a Wall Street bank, he had connections all over the world. It was always interesting to have dinner at the Grays', especially when I met this one fella who was becoming famous for his exploration and discoveries in the deserts of Sinkiang, commonly called the Gobi Desert, where he had found some intact dinosaur eggs of geological and archeological importance. Hearing about his treks through the desert to the foothills of the Himalayas near the north side of K2 instilled in me an ambition to visit that part of the world. Adding to my curiosity was the knowledge that my grandfather had originated from somewhere east of Lake Baykal on the edge of the Mongolian Desert.

Glenn and I took Prentice up the Exum Route. As we were walking up the wide ledge approaching Glenn's leap, the walls above and below us gave Glenn an idea. "Mr. Gray," Glenn said, "we ought to name this Wall Street."

"It looks something like Wall Street," Mr. Gray said. "And it may be damn near as dangerous."

***

I took up a fella once who had climbed some in Switzerland. Those people who came out from Switzerland and had used Swiss guides were the ones who were sometimes difficult for us. Glenn used to say, "If they say they've climbed the Matterhorn, take along some extra rope." Because people went over there and they were hauled up the mountain and hauled back. The guides didn't tell them a damn thing about technique; that was part of their system.

Like W. C. Field's famous saying, "Never wise up a sucker." You could cheat him out of his money, but never wise him up or teach him how you did it. The Swiss guides didn't want people climbing on their own; they wanted the business. The way mountaineering started in Switzerland was that the English aristocracy vacationed there, and some of them started to climb. Huts were built in the high pastures for them to stay in, and the guides would cook their meals and serve them. The guides never sat down with their clients and ate; that would have been socially unacceptable. By the time I arrived there, this sort of convention was just starting to be broken.

My new guiding philosophy not only meant being better prepared for the mountaineering aspects of guiding, but also included being better equipped socially to interact with clients. I knew how packers and guides were considered by the dudes and easterners who hired them. They thought local guides were great outdoorsmen and they enjoyed bringing them back to New York to show to their friends. But they were never social equals. There was always a barrier.

I was determined to take people up the mountain as equals and friends. I would learn from them and they would learn from me. I would be paid, but I would be more of a friend and a companion than a hired hand. I never liked being stigmatized by the terms *guide* and *packer*.

Anyway, this fella came from Switzerland and wanted to climb the Grand Teton. I didn't have anyone else to take on the trip so I agreed to take him up alone. All the way up he was telling me how the Swiss guides did things. Anything that I did that was any different from them he would tell me about in a tone that indicated he didn't think I was up to par with the Swiss guides. If I would take him up a line that I knew was the safest, he would say, "Why didn't we go that way? That looks safer and easier."

He was that way all the way to the top and on the way down too. I had to be very careful about belaying him, because I would want him to go a certain way and he would pick another route and would get himself into trouble. I was getting very annoyed, but, of course, I had to keep my cool. Finally, we got down to the Lower Saddle. From there I decided to go down a steep snow slope rather than descend some rocks that were quite loose. I could glissade or run down the snow slope and, if I fell, stop myself with an ice ax. I could do that safely, but I knew that he couldn't.

When we got there I said, "Let's put on the rope," but he said he didn't need a rope, that he'd been down steeper slopes in Switzerland. I told him it would be much safer if we roped up. There was a little run out at the bottom of the slope, but there was a chance a person could be hurt severely if he lost control or started rolling. There were a few rocks in the middle of the snow, and I remembered Tepee's accident.

But no, he didn't need the rope. Finally, in order to get the rope on him I lied to him. I told him it was a park rule that I had to rope up at this place and if I didn't, I might lose my license. Reluctantly, he allowed me to put the rope on him. So I got in a belaying position and told him to start. But instead of belaying I just took the end of the rope and wrapped it around a rock and looked up at a lone eagle that was sailing above the Tetons and didn't pay much attention to him.

I thought I knew what would happen and it did. Pretty soon the rope was played out and it started going out fast and I heard a grunt. He had gotten partway down, had fallen, and had slid down very fast until he hit the end of the rope, where he was stopped suddenly. Maybe the rope squeezed the air out of his lungs, but it certainly squeezed some of his ego out of him too. For the rest of the way down the mountain maybe he was angry, but he was contrite. That was the first and only time in my life that I ever did something to a climber that might cause him some discomfort.

***

Training and selecting guides was difficult. I soon found that some of the people who were the most agile and experienced climbers were not suitable guides. While taking people up the mountain they were thinking mostly of themselves, what they wanted to climb, how they wanted to climb, and the different chimneys and snow slopes they wanted to try. It turned into a climb that pleased them, and the clients were just along for the ride.

In my opinion, they should have been doing the type of climb that was best for the client. I soon learned that selfish people didn't make good guides. I once took a chance on a fella who I knew was inherently selfish, because he was such a good climber and could carry on good conversation and do almost everything a guide had to be able to do. I asked him to take a married couple up the Grand Teton, which he did, but he took a friend along. That would have been all right, but he didn't tell me in advance.

They did very well making it to the top, but when they got back down to the Upper Saddle, they asked the clients if they would mind if they waited a few minutes while they tried to climb a pinnacle near Tepee's Glacier. The couple probably wanted to get on down, but out of courtesy they said yes, they would rest awhile. Well, after an hour and a half of these people sitting out there in the wind, the guide came back and brought them down. The people weren't very pleased, and I never used him again as a guide. I didn't tell him why because he was a good friend and a good mountain climber. But he was a putrid guide.

A good guide sometimes had to be creative with difficult clients. We had one lady, a professor from Stanford, who talked continuously. When you climbed with her, you also went with her on dozens of other climbs that she had made throughout the world. You had to climb all those mountains in detail before you even reached timberline.

The guides talked about it all the time. Although she was charming and wonderful and always gave a liberal tip, people didn't want to listen to that continuous yakking. So no one wanted to take her.

At that time I was trying to teach the guides and convince them that their endurance could be enhanced and their fatigue could be lessened by rhythmic breathing. One of the guides got the idea that he'd take the professor up and teach her rhythmic breathing and energy conservation all the way up. If she breathed in rhythm, he said, she couldn't talk at the same time.

***

I once guided a scientist, and it was interesting to hear him talk. He worked for the Eastman Kodak Company, and I concluded from his conversation that he was one of the leading scientists working on the development of new kinds of film. He made some climbs with me in the Wind Rivers and he did fairly well, but he always wanted to go with just me and no one else along. One day he told me he wanted to do one of the most difficult guided climbs up the East Ridge of the Grand Teton. He seemed to have an unexplainable desire to face danger. I said I'd take him.

We camped at Amphitheater Lake and left early in the morning. We circumvented the Molar Tooth, went through the crack where I had spent the horrible night in 1924, and got to a place below a big chockstone where above it there was a pretty slick move on the rocks. It was climbable, but there weren't any real footholds or handholds that would support your whole weight. It took a little intuition to make sure that with all the holds combined you had 100 percent friction against the rock.

I climbed up a rather long lead and got securely behind a rock. I didn't have any pitons to belay with but I had a good place to belay from. The scientist started to climb up and slipped and slid down three or four feet before I stopped him by the belay. Well, suddenly he became another person from another world. He was frantic. He looked at me with a stare that nobody in Hollywood could duplicate.

Instead of climbing up the rope, he just took ahold of it and, with more strength than I thought he had, just pulled his body up hand over hand. That meant there was a loop of rope behind him and I knew that if he let go of the rope there I couldn't stop him until he had dropped all the way down past the loop to the end of the rope. By that time his momentum would have become so great that he probably would have jerked me right out of my belay, and we would have both ended up down on Tepee's Glacier.

He hand-over-handed right up to me and reached out and grabbed me with talon fingers and wild eyes. Maybe sometime in my reading I had learned how people who become frantic or out of control could be brought back to reality with a slap in the face, I don't know. Instinctively, I gave him a slap across his cheek. That made him angry and immediately he was rational.

So we climbed up to the top of the Grand Teton and down, but our relationship had cooled a little. I didn't apologize. Our conversation for the rest of the trip was a little strained.

I was married then and living with my wife in our tepee at Jenny Lake. He was camped nearby and he talked to my wife later about this incident and about how sorry he was that it had happened. He told her his life story, perhaps thinking that she would tell me. All his life he had had terrific fears. He was afraid of the night; even at the campground he had to be in his sleeping bag before it was too dark. He also had periods of terrific migraine headaches. One of the reasons he was climbing mountains was so he could get rid of this terrible fear complex he had, which he thought caused his headaches.

My wife told me, and I wasn't quite sure about his theory. But he had gone before I got back, and I never saw him again. I may have told Glenn that story but no one else. I didn't want it to get around, because I didn't want the park personnel or other mountaineers to think I was beating up my clients.

***

In the early days before Jackson's Hole was popular, people went to Banff. The Canadians had built railroads across Canada, and the railroad company had developed popular tourist destinations. Banff and Lake Louise were well-known centers to view breathtaking mountain panoramas, lakes, and big glaciers. Some people were coming there to climb, especially people from the eastern establishment who had become acquainted with climbing in Switzerland.

The railroad customarily had some Swiss guides in residence to guide tourists on the glaciers and to the tops of some peaks. Of course, no one in America at that time felt there were any Americans who were capable of guiding people on mountains like the guides from Switzerland. There were dude ranchers and packers and guides, but no one with a reputation as a mountaineering guide.

Sometime in the late twenties, a man from the American Alpine Club came to camp at Jenny Lake to wait for his daughter to arrive from Canada, where she had been climbing with one of the Swiss guides. He'd gone a day to our climbing school, and was looking forward with great anticipation to climbing the Grand Teton with his daughter. It was one of the great mountaineering things they were going to be able to do together. You could see he was looking forward to it as a major father-daughter event.

But when she arrived she was a far cry from the daughter who was looking forward to climbing the Grand Teton with her father. She announced almost immediately she did not want to climb the Grand at all. I was disappointed, because I was looking forward to the climb, and I was expecting not only the regular fee but maybe a little tip. Her father didn't want to force the issue. He was just very disappointed when he told me. He didn't know whether he wanted to climb without her or not.

That evening I went over to their camp at Jenny Lake. I thought with a little talk I could get her to go with him. So I was telling her what a wonderful climb it would be and I thought that she'd find it very, very interesting. She said, "No, I don't want to climb the Grand Teton. I made a climb in Canada that makes me eligible for the American Alpine Club. I don't need to climb the Grand Teton."

Evidently, she didn't like climbing in Canada either but she wanted to be in the American Alpine Club. So she endured the mountains until she had enough peaks collected to get in. It was from her and other people like her that we started to use the term peak collector for people who didn't climb for fun but climbed to build a résumé.

Over the years we came up with monikers for certain types of climbers like peak collectors and five-niners. Some five-niners wanted everyone to know they were five-niners. They had to carry quite a few pitons along for their climbs and lots of times they held the pitons on their belts and fastened them together. It created a Santa Claus jingle-bell effect. They'd wear them to Jackson to the bars to show off, and that's when I started calling them "piton janglers." Soon all the bartenders in town caught on to that name too.

***

Everyone had their reasons for climbing, whether it was peak collecting or something I did called "planting seeds." In Switzerland it was permissible and sort of a ritual for guides to take along a small bottle of wine. At the top, they opened this wine up with lunch. It was a sort of toast and a little bit of a celebration. So after prohibition we got in the habit, once in a while, of taking a couple bottles of beer up to the top of the Grand. We'd open them up there and give everyone a couple swallows of beer. It was a celebration and a conversation piece because it was something they didn't expect.

Once, when we were going up and we didn't have much to carry, I put several bottles of beer in my pack and took them up and hid them under a rock. Of course, it was summer and I knew they wouldn't freeze hard enough to break. This way, on occasions, I could pull out a beer to give to somebody who I knew wouldn't be offended.

One time, I was up there and was sort of joking. I didn't expect to make any money out of it and I said, "Boy, a bottle of beer would taste good now, wouldn't it? I'd give ten dollars for a bottle of beer." The other fella I was up there with said, "I would too." So I pulled out a bottle. We all laughed, but when we got down to the bottom and he paid his bill, he said, "There's the ten dollars for that beer."

So it became sort of a joke and a moneymaker. We called it "planting seeds," because if we could plant one bottle on top and sell it for ten dollars it was like a seed. Then we could go to Jackson for the harvest where it grew into several bottles of beer.

EPILOGUE

My earliest recollections of mountains are from adventure books — and I don't know what books they were — that my sister gave me to read when I was a kid. She was my schoolteacher in my early youth and developed my almost abnormal desire to learn from reading and to connect what I read with the reality of my life at the time, which I always seemed to do. I remember seeing pictures of real mountains that I presume were the Alps, because the Alps were the mountains that Americans were interested in, and that's where people climbed. There was some mountain climbing taking place in America when I was a kid, but it wasn't a sport.

After World War I, when my second oldest brother came back from the trenches of France and Germany, my family decided to sell out our farming interest in Iowa and go to Idaho to join my older brother as potato raisers instead of corn raisers. I looked forward with great anticipation to the railroad trip we were going to make all the way from Iowa to Idaho. I was excited during those preparations of loading our livestock and furniture into boxcars to ship and making huge baskets of fried chicken and cookies to eat on the train.

But my great anticipation was the realization that I was going to see mountains like the Swiss Alps I'd seen in pictures and, even at the age of nine, somehow had in my mind. Of course, I also had the stories of the early explorers of America, the ones who came West, and not only the immigrants who came West but also Indians who lived there. My uncle was a missionary for the Crow Indians, and I had seen some Indians whom he brought through Iowa on his lecture tours, dressed up in their supposedly Indian dress.

But as we rattled and clunked through the rest of Iowa and through Nebraska and even out through Cheyenne, Wyoming, and through Laramie, Wyoming, and on and on and on through the sagebrush of Wyoming where I-80 now runs, there were hills but no mountains, no steep cliffs covered with ice and snow. When we went through some larger hills and canyons as we came into the edge of Idaho, where there were hot springs and pools and things, there still weren't mountains that satisfied me.

Finally, when we got to our new home on the banks of the Snake River Canyon just north of Twin Falls, Idaho, I had an opportunity for an entirely new kind of life that was the answer to my thirst for adventure. Way in the distance to the north, I could see the snowcapped Sawtooth Mountains. In the fall, I watched them becoming more white and more white, further and further down. In the spring I watched the white melting upward and upward until in the summer only a few white spots were left in the distance. These were the places that drew me and where I wanted to go.

Meanwhile, I had to keep up with my four older brothers, who were not only farmers and ranchers now, but were sportsmen. They all hunted and trapped and fished, and in order to do that we had to climb down the very steep walls, one thousand feet down to the waters of the Snake River, which had worn an almost perpendicular canyon through the lava beds. Just up the stream a small distance were the roaring waters of Shoshone Falls that dropped down many, many feet further than Niagara Falls. Just a few miles above them were the famous Twin Falls. The river was split in the middle by a rock, and the two comparatively equal waterfalls were as high as Niagara Falls as well. Right below our ranch was Pillar Falls, rapids where fishing was supreme, and along the banks were animals to trap and furs to gather. This canyon soon became my playground.

My desire to go see the Sawtooth Mountains was finally answered when I was about thirteen. A friend of mine was invited to come up and spend some time with one of the rich ranchers who had a summer home near Ketchum, Idaho, an area that is now called Sun Valley. My mother was very understanding in letting me do things and she agreed to let me take old

Shorty, a gentle horse we had, and hitch him to a chaise of an old buggy. I loaded up the buggy with homemade bread and homegrown potatoes and onions and maybe a few cans of fruit and some flour to make biscuits, and sugar, salt, and pepper. The two of us got in this buggy with our dog Ranger and headed for the snowcapped Sawtooths.

It was quite a trip. We had to go down the hairpin-turn road that was dug out of solid rock to above Shoshone Falls, where they had a cable across the river and we could cross on the ferry, go up the north side of the canyon, and then go through one hundred or so miles of lava beds up toward Ketchum. Of course, the roads were absolutely unimproved. They just happened. The difficulty was the dust. It was awful. Every time the horse put its foot down, a huge amount of dust would sail up. So we were practically traveling in dust all day long depending on whether the wind was blowing and which way.

We were stopped by the sheriff in Shoshone, Idaho. We had to convince him that we really had permission from our folks to go and that we had the name of somebody we were going to visit up in Ketchum, before he would turn us loose. We got up to our friends' and stayed there a few days. Then we followed a stream up into the hills where we could catch more fish. Trout fishing was wonderful, and we lived off potatoes and trout. There were mountains there, and from where we camped in the valley we spent all day climbing up to the top of some of the peaks. Some of them were even above timberline, where there were rocky slopes on top. But no glaciers and no snowcapped mountains. There were some hidden over the hills to the north, but we didn't get that far into the Sawtooths. Those kind of mountains were limited in the Sawtooths anyway. They do not have big glaciers and only a few maintain snow all summer long.

So I didn't realize my dream of seeing mountains like I thought mountains should look until I rounded the curve of the country road near Rexburg, Idaho, and saw the Teton peaks in the distance with their snow and glaciers and their steeplelike tops that even surpassed my imagination and the pictures I had seen in my youth.